HAMPTON-BROWN

HIGH POINT

SUCCESS IN LANGUAGE • LITERATURE • CONTENT

Practice Book

LEVEL B

HAMPTON-BROWN

Practice Book Contents

UNIT 1 MIND MAP

Communication

DIRECTIONS Use the mind map to tell about the ways people communicate. Add more examples to the map as you read the selections in this unit.

Temporary		Lasting			
spoken words		newspaper			

Verbal		Nonverbal			
spoken words		pictures			

The Way I See It . . .

DIRECTIONS Circle each complete sentence.
Add periods to the sentences.

1. (The painting is interesting.)

2. The town in the background

3. A woman dances gracefully

4. Smiles in a sweet way

5. The countryside looks peaceful

DIRECTIONS Turn each subject or predicate into a
complete sentence. Tell about the painting.

6. uses shapes in an interesting way _The artist uses_

   shapes in an interesting way.

   _____

7. the little tree _____

   _____

   _____

8. the sky over the houses _____

   _____

   _____

9. reminds me of a dream _____

   _____

   _____

10. smile at each other _____

    _____

> **Complete Sentences**
>
> A **complete sentence** has a subject and a
> predicate.
>
> <u>A little town</u> <u>is in the background.</u>
>   subject   predicate
>
> The **complete subject** includes all the words that
> tell about the subject.
>
> <u>**A little tree**</u> is in the foreground.
>
> The **complete predicate** includes all the words in
> the predicate.
>
> A woman on a stool **milks a cow**.

I and the Village, Marc Chagall, oil on canvas. Copyright © 1911.

"I and the Village *is a Cubist fairy tale
that weaves dreamlike memories of
Russian folk tales, Jewish proverbs,
and the Russian countryside into one
glowing vision.*"

— H. W. Janson

MORE ABOUT COMPLETE SENTENCES Write three complete sentences that
tell what you think about the painting.

Words About Communication

New Words

attention

concentrate

creativity

experience

inspired

inventive

memory

motive

routine

Relate Words

DIRECTIONS Use the new words to complete the webs.
Some words can be used in both webs.

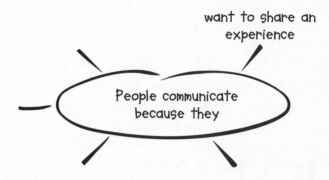

want to share an experience

People communicate because they

pay attention to every word

To be a good writer, you must

DIRECTIONS Write a sentence about each web.

1. _____

_____

_____

2. _____

_____

_____

Communicate with Nouns

DIRECTIONS Circle each noun in the passage.
Then write each noun in the correct column.
Write each noun only one time.

> ### Common and Proper Nouns
>
> A **noun** names a person, place, thing, or idea.
>
> A **common noun** names any person, place, thing, or idea.
>
> > A **boy** writes a **poem**.
>
> A **proper noun** names one particular person, place, thing, or idea.
>
> > **Saeed** writes a poem.

(Saeed) visited Iran last August. He went to a (game) with his brother, Toraj. They watched the national team play basketball. Over and over, he watched the players drop the ball into the basket. Saeed was stunned by their talent.

On the plane back to the United States, he wrote a poem about the players. He named the poem "Poetry in Motion" and gave it to his teacher. Mr. Gonzales sent it to the editor of the local newspaper. *The Gazette* published it and made Saeed a local star!

Common Nouns	Proper Nouns
1. _____ game _____	15. _____ Saeed _____
2. _____	16. _____
3. _____	17. _____
4. _____	18. _____
5. _____	19. _____
6. _____	20. _____
7. _____	21. _____
8. _____	22. _____
9. _____	
10. _____	
11. _____	
12. _____	
13. _____	
14. _____	

GRAMMAR: SINGULAR AND PLURAL NOUNS

Nouns: Some Change, Some Don't!

DIRECTIONS Complete the chart with words from the box. Follow the directions for each part of the chart.

farmer	spoon	honesty	love
hamburger	bunny	cookie	clothing
kangaroo	mermaid	lunch	furniture
luck	attention	scientist	thunder
forest	creativity	giraffe	shopper

Singular and Plural Nouns

A **singular noun** names one thing.
A **plural noun** names more than one thing.

A **poet** writes **poems**.
singular   plural

For nouns that name things you can count, add an ending to make it plural. For nouns you cannot count, use the same form to show both singular and plural.

Poetry uses **words** to communicate.
noncount   count
noun   noun

Write four singular count nouns.	Change four other count nouns to plural.	Write four noncount nouns.
1. _____	5. _____	9. _____
2. _____	6. _____	10. _____
3. _____	7. _____	11. _____
4. _____	8. _____	12. _____

DIRECTIONS Write a paragraph to tell about Gary Soto and his writing. Use count nouns and at least three noncount nouns. Trade your paragraph with a partner. Have your partner check that you used the correct form for each noun.

_____

_____

_____

_____

_____

_____

Poet and novelist Gary Soto works at his desk.

Find Poetry Anywhere!

DIRECTIONS Follow the steps to write a poem in free verse.

1 Find Words Read the newspaper story. Underline powerful words or phrases.

> ### Lions Trounce Tigers
>
> Friday night was a <u>night of firsts</u> for the Lakeshore Lions. It was the first huge win for the new coaching staff. The team wore their royal purple and gold uniforms for the first time. Lion Leo Moras took control as quarterback for his first start of the season. Passes sailed through the air to three new receivers.
>
>
> Leo Moras
>
> The Lions pounded the Tigers in a 28-6 victory. "This shows that we came to play," Coach Butler said, "It was a solid win against a strong Tiger defense."
>
> It looks like the Lions' season is off to a roaring start.

2 Write and Arrange Lines Put the underlined words together into lines. Arrange the lines until they look like a poem. Give the poem a title.

Write Lines ➡️ **Create a Poem**

                                                  Title: _____

   night of firsts _____   _____

_____   _____

_____   _____

_____   _____

_____   _____

3 Revise Your Poem Use the revising and editing steps of the writing process on Handbook pages 410–412 to improve your poem.

4 Share Poetry Read or recite your poem for the class.

Free Verse

Poetry uses powerful words that appeal to the senses. The words create clear pictures and express strong feelings.

Free verse is poetry that may not have regular rhyme or rhythm.

Visualize and Summarize

DIRECTIONS Make a web for each poem. Write the words that create strong images in your mind. Then write a sentence or two to summarize the poem.

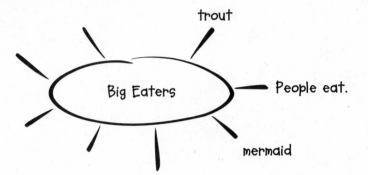

1. _____
   _____
   _____
   _____
   _____

2. _____
   _____
   _____
   _____
   _____

3. _____
   _____
   _____
   _____

4. Which poem creates the strongest image in your mind? Discuss the images with a partner.

Recognize Mood

> **Mood**
>
> The feeling you get from a poem or story is its **mood**. The mood can be happy, sad, excited, angry, or any other feeling.

DIRECTIONS Work in a group of three to create stories.

1 **Choose Words** Write your name for one set of mood words.

Mood Words

Set 1: _____ (Name)		Set 2: _____ (Name)		Set 3: _____ (Name)	
strolled	waved	trudged	clutched	skipped	chewed
gentle	bare arms	howling	worn coat	purple	popcorn
kissed	friendly	battered	fierce	tickled	fuzzy
softly	grin	heavily	shudder	happily	giggle

2 **Complete the Story** Write words to complete the story. Use the words in the order they appear in your set.

The Man on the Road

A man _____ along the road. A _____

wind _____ his face. He sighed _____ as he

_____ his _____ . Suddenly he saw a

_____ beast rushing toward him. "What shall I do now?" he

cried with a _____ .

---

3 **Read and Discuss the Stories** Read your story to your group. Compare the moods of the stories.

4 **Tell the Mood** Write the mood of your story.

Mood: _____

Words to Remember

New Words

history

legacy

memento

memorial

monument

mural

portray

represent

tribute

Relate Words

DIRECTIONS Work with a partner. Review the definitions of the new words in your book. Write an example of each kind of message. Then check the boxes that apply.

Messages:	Mural	Monument	Memento
Examples:	workers' mural		

	Mural	Monument	Memento
Does it portray people and places?			
Does it provide a legacy?			
Is it a memorial?			
Does it represent an event in history?			
Does it honor a living person or people?			

Use New Words in Context

DIRECTIONS Use the new words to write sentences. You may use more than one new word in a sentence.

1. _____

_____

2. _____

_____

3. _____

_____

4. _____

_____

5. _____

_____

SUM IT UP

Relate Main Ideas and Details

DIRECTIONS Complete the main idea diagram for each topic from "Talking Walls." Then write two paragraphs on a separate sheet of paper. Tell about one topic in each paragraph.

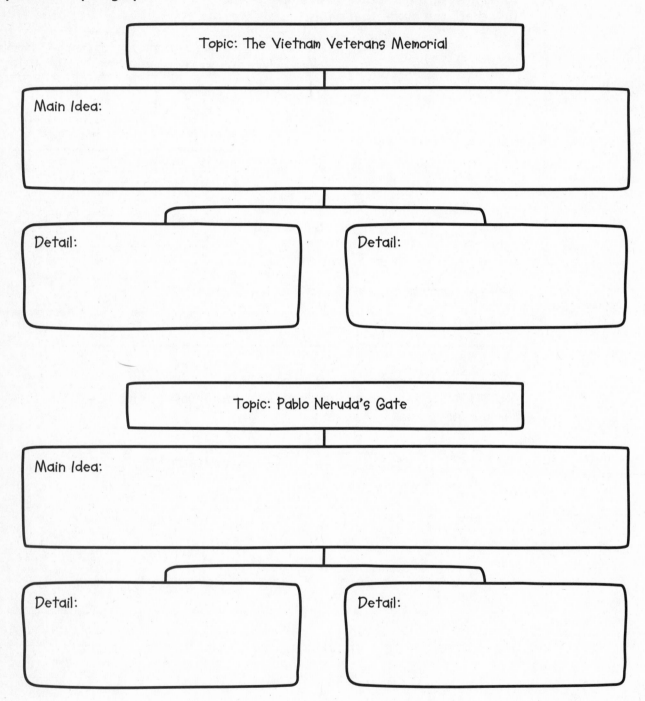

Topic: The Vietnam Veterans Memorial

Main Idea:

Detail:

Detail:

Topic: Pablo Neruda's Gate

Main Idea:

Detail:

Detail:

The Walls Still Talk

Subjects and Predicates

The **complete subject** includes all the words that tell about the subject. The **simple subject** is the most important word in the complete subject.

Many people like Pablo Neruda's poetry.

The **complete predicate** includes all the words in the predicate. The **simple predicate** is the verb.

Some admirers **write** tributes to him.

DIRECTIONS Circle the simple subject in each sentence. Underline the simple predicate.

1. Diego Rivera's (paintings) have strong lines and bold colors.

2. His murals decorate walls in Mexico.

3. The large pictures show important events in Mexican history.

4. Ordinary Mexican people appear in the murals.

5. Their lives were important to Diego Rivera.

6. People around the world appreciate Diego Rivera's work.

DIRECTIONS Think about "Talking Walls." Complete the sentences. Trade with a partner. Have your partner circle the simple subjects and underline the simple predicates.

7. The (walls) in the essay _tell stories in words and pictures_____ .

8. Colorful murals _____ .

9. Diego Rivera's murals _____ .

10. _____ tell future generations about us.

11. _____ names Americans who died in the Vietnam War.

12. One Chilean poet _____ .

13. _____ honor the poet's memory.

14. _____ send messages across time.

Use Context Clues

DIRECTIONS Look at each bold word. Underline the signal words and context clue. Then write the meaning of the word.

> ### Context Clues
> One type of **context clue** gives you an **example** for the new word. Look for the signal words *and, like,* or *as.*
>> The artist used pastel colors **like light blue and pink.**
>
> Another type of context clue gives you a **contrast** for the new word. Look for the signal words *but, not, however,* or *instead.*
>> The artist used pastel colors **instead of bright colors.**

1. Rivera had **tremendous** energy <u>and worked long hours</u> every day.

   tremendous = ___*a large amount of*___

2. Rivera's murals might show farming, cooking, or some other **occupation**.

   occupation = _____

3. The Vietnam Veterans Memorial is **glossy** instead of dull.

   glossy = _____

4. The Vietnam Veterans Memorial touches **emotions**, like sadness and loss.

   emotions = _____

5. Pablo Neruda loved poetry but his father **scorned** it.

   scorned = _____

DIRECTIONS Use a context clue to find the meaning of each bold word in the passage. Then tell what kind of clue you used.

	Meaning of Word	Kind of Clue
Art in Our Town Our town has lots of **statues**, like stone rabbits and horses. One shows a **military hero**. She looks like a brave soldier or sailor. Her clothes are **drab**, but one shoe is bright. This is because people **repeatedly** rub her toe every time they pass by. This statue is **unique**; it is not like any other.	_____ _____ _____ _____ _____	_____ _____ _____ _____ _____

Using the Dictionary

DIRECTIONS Study the dictionary entry. Then use a dictionary to complete the chart. Identify the part of speech for each underlined word. Write the definition for it.

The **base word** is the basic form of the word.

The **definition** tells what the word means.

The **part of speech** shows how the word can be used in a sentence. Abbreviations for parts of speech:

adj.	adjective	*n.*	noun
adv.	adverb	*prep.*	preposition
conj.	conjunction	*pron.*	pronoun
interj.	interjection	*v.*	verb

The **pronunciation** shows how to say the word.

labor *noun* **1.** Hard work: *It took months of labor to dig the tunnel.* **2.** Working people or their union representatives: *Labor supported the bill in Congress.*
◊ *verb* **1.** To work hard: *We labored to learn our lines in the school play.* **2.** To move or act with great effort; struggle: *The train labored up the steep slope.*
la•bor (lā′bər) ◊ *noun, plural* **labors** ◊ *verb* **labored, laboring**

A **sample sentence** is an example of how to use the word.

An entry shows any **plural forms** or other **verb forms** for the word.

	Word	Base Word	Part of Speech	Definition
1.	Americans **labored** and fought **bravely** in the Vietnam War.	labor	verb	to work hard
2.	Many **soldiers** were killed.			
3.	Maya Lin **designed** a memorial to honor them.			
4.	Their names were **chiseled** into granite.			
5.	People leave flowers and **messages** by the wall.			
6.	The monument is the **greatest** tribute to those who died.			

Wordless Messages

Compound Sentences

A **compound sentence** is made up of two independent clauses. The clauses are joined by a **comma** and a **conjunction**.

> Cave drawings are beautiful, **and** they tell about the past.

The conjunction **and** shows that the two ideas are alike. **But** shows that two ideas are different, and **or** shows a choice between ideas.

DIRECTIONS Work with a partner. Choose *and, but,* or *or* to join each pair of sentences. Write the sentences. Circle the conjunctions.

1. Early Americans left us messages.
   They did not leave them in writing.

   Early Americans left us messages, (but) they did

   not leave them in writing.

2. Native Americans drew images on rock walls. They carved images into rocks.

   _____

   _____

3. You can view the drawings in Canyon de Chelly in Arizona. You can study the carvings

   at Mesa Verde in Colorado. _____

   _____

4. Visitors may look at the drawings. They may not touch them.

   _____

   _____

5. The images are very old. The Native Americans want to protect them.

   _____

   _____

Images on rock walls send messages across time.

6. These messages across time may not be in words. They communicate

   their messages powerfully! _____

   _____

Words About Village Life

New Words

grain

granary

harvest

kernel

kingdom

palace

plantation

storyteller

village

villager

Relate Words

DIRECTIONS Write each new word where it belongs in the chart.

People	Places	Things	Actions
storyteller	palace		

Use New Words in Context

DIRECTIONS With a partner, brainstorm story events that could go with each title. Use the new words to write a story summary.

1. **The King Who Sank in the Grain:** King Fred falls into the palace granary and is buried in grain! The villagers run from the plantation to get him out.

2. **Yam Harvest Time:** _____

_____

_____

3. **The Silly Storyteller:** _____

_____

_____

4. **No Grain for Mario:** _____

_____

_____

Sun Girl and Moon Boy

DIRECTIONS Complete each sentence. Add articles where they are needed. See Handbook page 435 for examples of nouns that do not need articles.

1. *The Sun Girl and the Moon Boy* is _____a_____ folk tale from _____ Korea.

2. _____ story is written in _____ English by _____ Yangsook Choi.

3. In this story, _____ mother tells her children not to open the door to strangers when she goes to market.

4. On her way back, she has _____ encounter with _____ evil tiger.

5. _____ tiger swallows _____ mother.

6. Then _____ tiger goes to _____ children's house.

7. The tiger pretends to be _____ mother of _____ children.

8. _____ frightened children plan _____ escape.

9. They race outside and climb up _____ tree in the garden.

10. When the tiger climbs after _____ children, _____ rope drops from above.

11. _____ children are pulled up into _____ sky.

12. _____ girl becomes _____ sun and _____ boy becomes the moon.

13. Together, the children bring sunlight and moonlight to _____ world.

14. They have _____ joyful reunion with their mother, who has turned into stars.

MORE ABOUT ARTICLES Write a paragraph about your favorite folk tale. Circle all the articles.

Articles

Use **the** before a noun that is specific.

The story is exciting.

Use **a** or **an** before a noun that is not specific. Use **a** before a word that starts with a consonant sound. Use **an** before a word that starts with a vowel sound.

It is **a** Korean tale. It is **an** old tale.

Some nouns do not take articles before them.

The tale is from **Korea**.

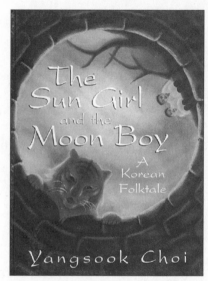

Some stories are told around the world. This tale is similar to the story of Red Riding Hood told in Europe.

A Delightful Storyteller!

DIRECTIONS Use the correct present tense form of the verb in parentheses to complete each sentence.

> **Present Tense**
>
> A **present tense verb** tells about an action that is happening now or an action that happens all the time.
>> The children **laugh**.
>> They **love** to hear stories.
>
> Present tense verbs must agree with the subject. To talk about one thing, add **s** to the verb.
>> The story **begins**.

1. Diane Ferlatte _____*tells*_____ stories to all kinds of audiences. (**tell**)

2. Diane _____ to tell African American and Creole stories. (**like**)

3. She _____ the stories she heard on her grandparents' porch in Louisiana. (**remember**)

4. She _____ warmth and excitement to these old tales. (**bring**)

5. Modern storytellers, like Diane, _____ costumes, lighting, and music to help tell the tale. (**use**)

6. They _____ the roles of the characters. (**perform**)

7. Storytellers _____ with the audience. (**connect**)

8. The audience _____ an experience with the storyteller. (**share**)

9. Diane _____ storytelling is a good way to pass on culture. (**think**)

10. Storytelling _____ young people use imagination. (**help**)

11. Good stories _____ young children for reading. (**prepare**)

12. Diane _____ that stories contribute to world peace. (**believe**)

13. Through stories, people _____ other cultures better. (**understand**)

14. Audiences _____ about different parts of the world. (**learn**)

15. Wherever storytellers go, they _____ people with their tales. (**delight**)

Professional storyteller Diane Ferlatte performs for audiences around the world.

Make Comparisons

DIRECTIONS Read "The Neighbor's Tale." Complete the Venn diagram to compare it to one of the folk tales in your book.

The Neighbor's Tale

Helena was an American farmer. She wanted to buy a plow horse from her neighbor, but she had no extra money.

The neighbor said, "If you can tell me a story that lasts forever, I'll give you a horse."

Helena smiled. "You have a deal," she said. "Here is a story that never ends.

"Once there was a family that lived by a lake. Every spring, water from a creek rushed down the hill into the lake.

"One year the lake overflowed. When the water reached the family's home, the father said, 'Daughter, we must empty this lake. Grab a bucket.'

"So the girl grabbed a bucket and dipped it into the lake water. She lugged the bucket of water to the top of the hill and dumped it into the creek. Then she went back down to the lake. She filled her bucket again. She lugged it up to the top of the hill…"

The neighbor laughed at the clever story. "Excellent!" she said. "The plow horse is yours, my friend."

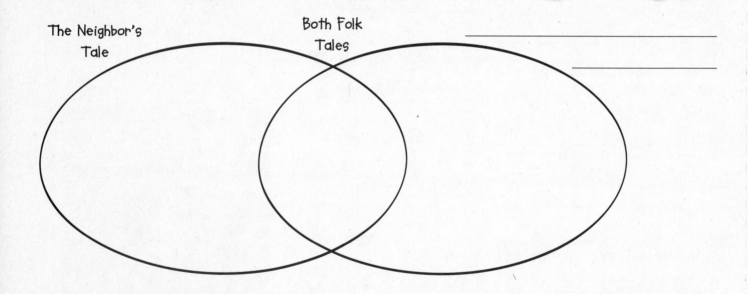

The Neighbor's Tale

Both Folk Tales

_____

DIRECTIONS Write a summary. Tell how the two folk tales are alike and how they are different.

_____

_____

_____

GRAMMAR: NOUNS

Out of Africa

DIRECTIONS Read the folk tale. Underline the common nouns each time they appear. Circle the proper nouns each time they appear.

> **Nouns**
>
> A **noun** names a person, place, thing, or idea.
>
> A **common noun** names any person, place, thing, or idea.
>   The **woman** told a **story**.
>
> A **proper noun** names a particular person, place, thing, or idea.
>   **Diane** told a story from **Africa**.
>
> **Specific nouns** give a clear picture of what you mean.
>   Jasmin shared a **legend** from **Ethiopia**.

The Wise Son

In (Africa,) in the <u>country</u> of Ghana, there once lived a man who had three sons. One day, before he left on a long journey, Kofi gathered his sons around him. He gave each child an egg. "I will be gone a long time," he told his sons. "Use these eggs to help your mother."

But as soon as Kofi left, the two older boys cooked and ate their eggs. The youngest boy, Ebo, gave his egg to his mother, who put it under a hen to hatch.

Many months later, Kofi returned. The youngest son prepared a great feast to welcome him back—for he had many chickens and many eggs.

DIRECTIONS Add common and proper nouns to create your own folk tale.

In the town of _____ , there was a _____ with three

daughters. The eldest daughter was named _____ . The middle daughter was

named _____ . The youngest was _____ .

The family lived in a _____ at the edge of the _____ . One day,

a _____ came to the door. He had many beautiful _____ for sale.

The daughters begged their mother to buy some.

The woman offered the man a golden _____ . Then she gave each daughter a

_____ . "Take good care of these," she warned her girls. Only _____

listened, and she had the joy of the beautiful _____ all her life.

It Goes On and On . . .

A Never-Ending Story
A story always has **characters**, a **setting**, and **events**. In a never-ending story, the last line of the story is repeated over and over.

DIRECTIONS Write a never-ending story.

1 **Plan a Story** Make a story map to show your characters, setting, and main events. Look on Handbook pages 375–377 for examples.

2 **Think of an Ending** Write something a character, or you as the storyteller, says over and over again to make the story never-ending.

3 **Write the Story** Now use your imagination to write a story that never ends!

Title: _____

Tell about the **setting** and **characters**.

The year was _____ . _____ and

_____ were at the _____

in _____ .

Describe the **events**. Tell what your characters did and said.

That day, _____

_____

_____ .

As a result, _____

_____

_____

_____ .

Consequently, _____

_____

_____

_____

_____ .

Write an **ending** that will make your story go on forever.

_____

_____

_____

_____ .

20

RESEARCH SKILLS

A Computerized Card Catalog

Computerized Card Catalog

A **computerized card catalog** has the same information as the cards in a card catalog. You can search for a book by typing in an author's name, a book title, a subject, or a key word.

DIRECTIONS Work with a partner. Use a computerized card catalog to find information about a topic.

1 Brainstorm topics related to bread. Write key words to look up.

Topic: _____

Key Words	References (books, videos, and audio recordings)

2 Do a subject search. Type in your key words. Follow the directions on the computer to see information about the references that interest you.

3 Find references that you think might be useful. Add them to the chart.

4 Compare results with your classmates. Discuss your answers to these questions.

1. What steps did you follow to find your references? _____

_____

_____

2. Which key words led to useful information? _____

3. Which references do you think are most useful? Why? _____

_____

_____

_____

© Hampton-Brown

CONTENT AREA CONNECTIONS

Learn About Grains and Diet

DIRECTIONS Research a grain. Follow the steps.

1 List all the grains you have eaten this past week. Think about each meal.

_____

2 Choose one grain to research. What do you want to know about it? Write your research questions.

_____

_____

3 Choose your sources. Write the titles or addresses.

☐ encyclopedia   ☐ science book   ☐ magazine   ☐ Web site

_____   _____   _____   _____

_____   _____   _____   _____

4 Find the answers to your questions. Take notes. Look on Handbook pages 394–396 for help.

How is corn prepared?

— boiled or roasted on the cob

— creamed or made into corn meal

5 Plan your report. Use your notes to decide what you will say. Choose what you will show.

☐ a real grain from the supermarket

☐ a drawing or photograph of the grain

☐ a video showing where the grain is grown

6 Review pages 401–402 in the Handbook. Then present your report to the class.

Wheat

© Hampton-Brown

Space Words

Relate Words

DIRECTIONS Check the two words in each box that go together. Use each pair of words in a sentence.

New Words

- cavity
- dentist
- filling
- invader
- invasion
- launch
- receive
- spaceman
- station
- stay tuned

dentist	invasion	invader
filling	cavity	stay tuned
launch	spaceman	station

1. _____

   _____

2. _____

   _____

3. _____

   _____

Use Context Clues

DIRECTIONS Write the new words that complete the sentences.

4. The _____ spaceman _____ in Dr. Ngo's office needs help.

5. An _____ of space germs has left a _____ in his tooth.

6. Only the galaxy's best _____ can help him now.

7. Dr. Ngo puts a _____ in some spaceman's mouth every day.

8. "I will _____ an attack on this tooth!" says Dr. Ngo.

9. The spaceman listens to horrible music on the radio _____ in Dr. Ngo's office.

10. Why does Dr. Ngo _____ to such bad music?

11. "Are you ready to _____ a brand new filling?" asks Dr. Ngo.

12. "Get this _____ out of my mouth!" yelps the spaceman. Dr. Ngo saves the day.

GRAMMAR: COMPOUND SENTENCES

The Great Tooth Mystery!

DIRECTIONS Circle the coordinating conjunction in each sentence.

1. Lee Chung did not believe in UFOs, (nor) did he believe in aliens.

2. Lee's mother was an astronaut, and Lee's grandfather was an astronomer.

3. Neither had seen life on other planets, nor had they heard voices.

4. Lee's opinion changed one night, for something odd happened.

> **Compound Sentences**
>
> An **independent clause** can stand alone as a sentence.
>> The volume faded.
>> The boy heard static.
>
> A **compound sentence** has two independent clauses joined by a **comma** and a **conjunction**.
>> The volume faded, **and** the boy heard static.

DIRECTIONS Combine each pair of independent clauses to form a compound sentence. Use each conjunction from the box at least once.

but	and	for
yet	or	

5. Lee could ignore the pain in his tooth. He could call his dentist.

_____

_____

6. Lee decided to call Dr. Kapp. His tooth would only get worse. _____

_____

7. The appointment wasn't bad. He still hated getting a filling. _____

_____

8. That night Lee fell into a deep sleep. He heard a strange message. _____

_____

9. He held his breath and listened. He couldn't figure it out. _____

_____

10. Then Lee remembered his filling. He realized it was tuning into outer space!

_____

_____

GRAMMAR: PRESENT TENSE

The Question of UFOs

DIRECTIONS Write *am*, *is*, or *are* to finish Anahita's essay.

Unidentified Flying Objects (UFOs) _____are_____
1.

a mystery. I like studying about UFOs; but, like many

people, I _____ not sure they exist.
2.

What _____ that strange object in the sky? Often the
3.

answer _____ easily explained. I _____ sure that
4.   **5.**

some UFOs _____ weather balloons. Some UFOs
6.

_____ probably military jets. Others _____ meteors
7.   **8.**

or swarms of insects!

Nonetheless, some people_____ sure that UFOs exist. They believe a UFO
9.

_____ a ship from another planet. The spaceship _____ full of visitors.
10.   **11.**

Hopefully, the visitors _____ friendly!
12.

Such ideas _____ not scientific. A scientist _____ only interested
13.   **14.**

in facts. However, some scientists think that UFOs _____ worthy of more study.
15.

My uncle _____ a scientist. Uncle Stefan _____ an expert about
16.   **17.**

UFOs and wants to see one. I _____ eager to see one, too. The idea
18.

_____ fascinating to me. For now, however, I _____ still not sure
19.   **20.**

that they exist.

by Anahita Benoit

Identify Events in the Plot

DIRECTIONS Read the story. Write the events in order on the story staircase map.

Clara and the Classroom Alien

Clara sat in her classroom. She felt a little tug on her shoe. She looked down. A purple alien with three eyes was standing on her foot! He was five inches tall.

"Help," he cried. Tears filled each eye.

Clara leaned over and pretended to clean her shoe. "How?" she whispered.

"I need to get outside. My ship is coming when your clock says 12."

Clara thought for a minute. It was almost time for lunch. "OK," she said. "I'll sneak you out. Don't worry."

Clara lifted the little man and tucked him into her pack.

"Clara!" said Ms. Trent. "Do you have something to share?" asked Ms. Trent. "Next time, your little friend goes into my desk. Is that clear?"

"Yes, ma'am," said Clara. She tried to look very busy writing.

The bell rang and Clara ran for the door. A purple streak shot from her pack. A ball of aluminum foil floated away in the wind. It was 12 noon.

Story Staircase Map

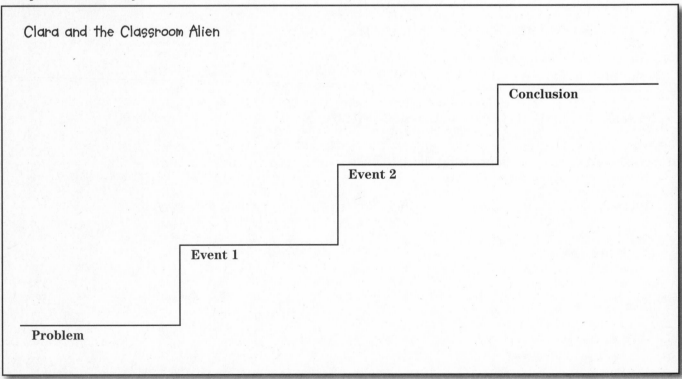

Clara and the Classroom Alien

Conclusion

Event 2

Event 1

Problem

© Hampton-Brown

GRAMMAR: VERBS

Fast Food Fast!

Verbs

An **action verb** tells what the subject does.
The spacemen **eat** potato pancakes.

A **linking verb** connects, or links, the subject to a word in the predicate. The word in the predicate describes or renames the subject.
Their pancakes **are** heavy.
Our breakfast **is** cereal.

The verb must always agree with the subject of the sentence.
The **spaceship lands** on Earth.
The **visitors seem** hungry.

DIRECTIONS Circle the verb in each sentence. Tell whether it is an action verb or a linking verb.

Kind of Verb

1. The spacemen (tumble) toward Earth. _____ action _____

2. They land in the middle of a mall. _____

3. They are huge and hungry. _____

4. One invader sees a hamburger shop. _____

5. Everyone runs toward it. _____

6. Soon the shop is crowded. _____

7. The fat men grab hundreds of hamburgers. _____

8. The customers are amazed at the sight. _____

DIRECTIONS Circle the linking verb in each sentence. Tell whether the word in the predicate describes or renames the subject.

9. The invaders (feel) hungry again. _____ describes the subject _____

10. The hamburgers are snacks. _____

11. They seem eager for more goodies. _____

12. The smells in the bakery are appealing. _____

13. Lunch is ready. _____

14. Pies and cakes are lunch. _____

Fat Men from Space
LEVEL B TE page T60

27

Unit 1 | Communication

RESEARCH SKILLS

Using an Encyclopedia

DIRECTIONS Work with a partner. Use an encyclopedia volume or an electronic encyclopedia to research a topic.

1 Choose a topic that interests you.

We want to know about _____ .

2 Look up the topic in an encyclopedia. Read the article. Then complete the notecard. See Handbook page 396 for help.

Notecard

Write a **research question**.

Write the **name** or the **Web address**.

Include the **page number**.

Write **facts** you learned from the article. Make sure they answer your research question.

Encyclopedia:

Article title:

Fact 1:

Fact 2:

3 Look for cross references. Find and read another article related to your topic. Write the title and one fact you learned.

Article title: _____

_____

Fact: _____

_____

_____

Cattle, goats, and many other animals that eat plants have bacteria in their digestive systems that break down cellulose. The bodies of such animals use the digested cellulose as food.   Richard A. Ahrens

Related articles in *World Book* include:

Bread	Glycogen	Saccharides
Cellulose	Nutrition	Starch
Dextrose	(Carbohy-	Sucrose
Glucose	drates)	Sugar

Cross references give a list of other subjects you can look up to find information related to a topic.

© Hampton-Brown

Analyze Your Diet

DIRECTIONS Keep track of the foods you eat for one day. Use the chart. Compare the number of servings you ate to those in the food pyramid. Write what you learned about your eating habits.

The Food Pyramid

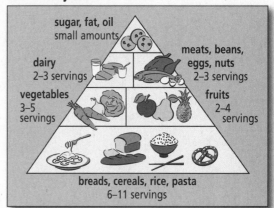

sugar, fat, oil
small amounts

dairy
2–3 servings

meats, beans,
eggs, nuts
2–3 servings

vegetables
3–5
servings

fruits
2–4
servings

breads, cereals, rice, pasta
6–11 servings

Number of Servings for One Day

	sugar, fat, oil	dairy	meat, beans, eggs, nuts	vegetables	fruits	breads, cereals, rice, pasta
Breakfast						
Snack						
Lunch						
Snack						
Dinner						
Total Servings						
Food Pyramid Servings	small amounts	2–3 servings	2–3 servings	3–5 servings	2–4 servings	6–11 servings

Analysis: _____

_____

_____

UNIT 2 MIND MAP

Belonging

DIRECTIONS Use the mind map to show your ideas about belonging. As you read the selections in this unit, add new ideas you learn about belonging.

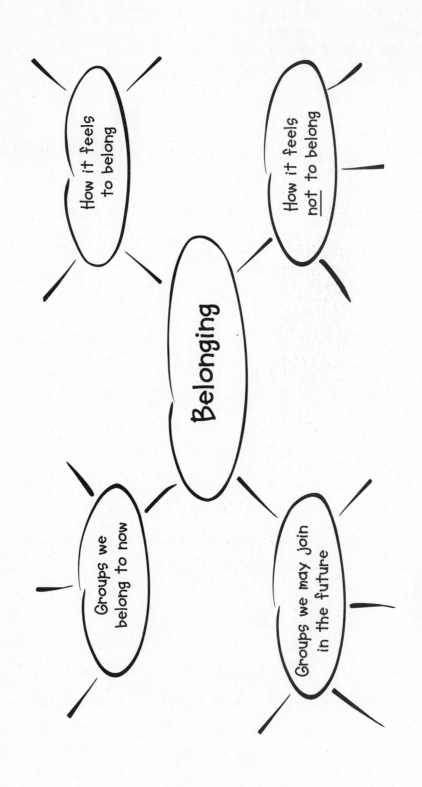

How it feels
to belong

How it feels
not to belong

Belonging

Groups we
belong to now

Groups we may join
in the future

Name _____ Date _____

Q and A

DIRECTIONS Use the questions to interview a family member or friend. Write the answers in complete sentences.

Person Interviewed: _____

1. Where do you live? _____

   _____

   _____

2. Did you move here from another country? If so, where did you

   live before? _____

   _____

3. What are your favorite activities? _____

   _____

4. What was something interesting you did this week? _____

   _____

5. How do you get to school or work? _____

   _____

6. What do you do on weekends? _____

   _____

7. What did you like to do as a young child? _____

   _____

8. What do you miss about where you used to live? _____

   _____

> ### Present and Past Tense
>
> A **present tense verb** tells about an action that is happening now or that happens all the time.
>
> > Rada **gets** on the bus.
> > She **takes** the bus every day.
>
> A **past tense verb** tells about an action that happened in the past. Regular past tense verbs end in **-ed**. Irregular past tense verbs do not.
>
> > Rada **stepped** off the bus.
> > She **took** her books with her.

MORE ABOUT THE PRESENT AND PAST TENSE Look back at the questions and answers in your interview. Circle the present tense verbs. Underline the past tense verbs.

Words for Special Days

New Words

- apron
- babushka
- bouquet
- bride
- celebrate
- engaged
- husband
- nightdress
- quilt
- tablecloth
- wedding huppa

Locate and Use Definitions

DIRECTIONS Work with a group. Predict where each new word belongs in the chart. Check each meaning in the Glossary. Correct the chart if you need to.

Weddings	Clothing	Household Objects
bride	apron	tablecloth

DIRECTIONS Use the new words to write sentences about each category in the chart.

Weddings:

1. _____

   _____

2. _____

   _____

Clothing:

3. _____

   _____

4. _____

   _____

Household Objects:

5. _____

   _____

6. _____

   _____

The Quilting Bee

DIRECTIONS Read the story. Look at the underlined verbs.

Henrietta <u>calls</u> to her daughter from the wide porch. Marcella <u>looks</u> up from the creek. "Yes, Mama?"

"The ladies will be here soon." Henrietta <u>goes</u> back inside the cool, tidy farmhouse. The scent of acorns <u>drifts</u> through the open windows. Henrietta <u>places</u> scraps of bright fabric on the dining room table, along with needles and thread.

Suddenly, heavy footsteps <u>rattle</u> on the porch. The ladies <u>rap</u> on the door. "We're here!" they <u>cry</u>.

Marcella <u>dashes</u> up the steps after the ladies. "I'm ready!" she <u>announces</u>, breathlessly.

Her mother <u>laughs</u>. "Go and wash up," she <u>commands</u>. "You can't sew with dirty hands."

> **Past Tense**
>
> A **past tense verb** tells about an action that happened earlier, or in the past.
>
> Long ago, Marcella **helped** her mother.
>
> Regular past tense verbs end in **–ed**. Follow the spelling rules to form the past tense.
>
> thread + –ed = thread**ed**   wrap + –ed = wrap**ped**
> place + –ed = plac**ed**   try + –ed = tri**ed**
>
> Irregular past tense verbs do not end in **–ed**.
> go = **went**   keep = **kept**

DIRECTIONS Rewrite the story. Change the underlined verbs to the past tense.

Henrietta called to her daughter from the wide porch.

_____

_____

_____

_____

_____

_____

_____

_____

_____

_____

_____

_____

Through the Generations

DIRECTIONS Complete each sentence. Use the past tense form of the verb. Look at the chart of irregular verbs on Handbook pages 450–451 if you need help.

1. Anna and her family ___came___ to America from Russia.
   come

2. They _____ to make a new life in New York City.
   have

3. Some members of the family _____ artificial flowers to sell.
   make

4. Anna's father _____ in a wagon and hauled things.
   ride

5. In school, Anna _____ to learn English.
   begin

6. When she _____ English words, they
   hear
   sounded strange to her.

7. Before long, she _____ how to speak English.
   know

8. When Anna _____ out of her dress, her
   grow
   mother cut it up to make a quilt.

9. She also used other old clothes that she _____ in a basket.
   keep

10. The quilt _____ very important in Anna's family.
    become

11. When Anna got married, her mother _____ her
    give
    the quilt as a wedding huppa.

12. The quilt _____ a family treasure.
    be

MORE ABOUT THE IRREGULAR PAST TENSE Choose a passage from a book that tells about the past. Write the irregular past tense verbs.

GRAMMAR: FUTURE TENSE

Pass It On!

DIRECTIONS Complete the paragraph. Use *will* with a main verb to form the future tense.

Mr. Gomez has a portrait of his mother. He

_____will hang_____ it in his new house.

1.

It _____ nice above the fireplace.

2.

The portrait _____ in a place of honor.

3.

Eventually, Mr. Gomez _____ the

4.

portrait to his son, Luis. In time, Luis _____

5.

it down to his children.

DIRECTIONS Complete the paragraph. Use *am going to, is going to,* or *are going to* to form the future tense.

My mother has some colorful scarves that her grandmother

embroidered. Because they are so pretty, we _____are going to_____

6.

keep them. Mother _____ cover the table with

7.

a blue one. She _____ let Michaela and I wear

8.

the others on special days. We _____ treat the

9.

scarves with care. One day, I _____ give my

10.

scarf to my daughter.

MORE ABOUT THE FUTURE TENSE Write about a real or imaginary family treasure. Use future tense verbs.

Retell Patricia's Family Story

DIRECTIONS A family tree shows the generations of a person's family. Read "The Keeping Quilt" again. Stop after each section to complete each generation of Patricia's family tree.

Patricia's Family Tree

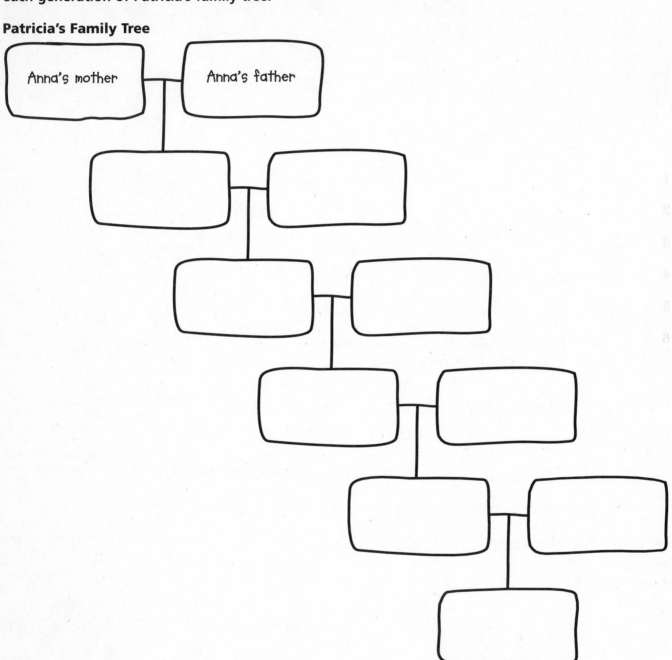

Anna's mother

Anna's father

MORE ABOUT PATRICIA'S STORY Use the family tree to retell the story to a partner. Tell how each generation used the quilt.

GRAMMAR: VERB TENSES

A Family Treasure

DIRECTIONS Underline the verb in each sentence.
Name the verb tense.

Some families pass on *Matroyshka*, or nesting dolls, as family treasures.

> ### Verb Tenses
>
> The **present tense** of a verb shows an action that is happening now or happens all the time.
>> She **folds** the beautiful old quilt.
>
> The **past tense** shows an action that happened in the past.
>> Her ancestors **made** the quilt.
>
> The **future tense** shows an action that will happen in the future.
>> In time, her daughter **will have** the quilt.

Verb Tense

1. Great-Grandpa Sasha <u>asked</u> for Anna's hand in marriage. ___past___

2. Anna accepted his proposal. _____

3. Anna and Sasha gave Carle the keeping quilt. _____

4. Today, Carle's granddaughter has the quilt. _____

5. She wrote a story about the quilt. _____

6. In her story, she tells the quilt's history. _____

7. One day, her daughter will take the quilt. _____

8. After many years, she is going to give it to her children. _____

9. It will have a place of honor in a new home. _____

10. It is a family treasure. _____

DIRECTIONS Write sentences to tell about family treasures.
Use verbs from the box in the past, present, and future tenses.

be	save	have
make	keep	repair
paint	give	inherit

11. **Past:** _I inherited a watch from my grandpa._

12. **Present:** _____

13. **Past:** _____

14. **Future:** _____

The Keeping Quilt
LEVEL B TE page T85

Unit 2 | Belonging

Using Parts of a Book

DIRECTIONS Work with a partner. Turn to each part of your book. Complete the sentences.

Title Page

1. The title of the book is _____High Point_____ .

2. The publisher is _____ .

3. The authors are _____

_____ .

There are pages at the front and back of your book that can help you find information.

Table of Contents

4. In Unit 1, "Tales Across Time" starts on _____ .

5. The selection "Teammates" in Unit 2 is a _____

written by Peter Golenbock.

6. In Unit 4, the Reading Strategy for "The Big Blast" teaches you how to

_____ .

7. All the selections in Unit 5 are about _____ .

8. The Index begins on _____ .

Index

9. On page 491, there are _____ entries for e-mail.

10. Find the **Grammar, Mechanics, Usage, and Spelling** section. You can learn more

about adverbs that compare if you go to _____ .

11. Find the **Research Skills** section. To find out how to take notes during the research

process, you can look on _____ .

12. You can find entries for the Internet under these sections:

_____ and _____ .

Synonyms and Antonyms

New Words

alike

common

delight

obvious

serious

thrive

unalike

variety

Relate Words

DIRECTIONS Write a synonym and an antonym for each new word.

Vocabulary	Choose from these words:			Synonym	Antonym
common	special	small	ordinary	ordinary	special
delight	show	please	anger		
obvious	clear	serious	hidden		
variety	size	likeness	difference		
thrive	grow	dry up	live		
alike	unalike	together	same		
serious	healthy	silly	thoughtful		

Use New Words in Context

DIRECTIONS Use a new word to write a sentence. Have a partner choose a synonym or an antonym for the new word and rewrite the sentence.

Example:

My mother had a serious look on her face.

My mother had a thoughtful look on her face.

My mother had a silly look on her face.

1. _____

_____

2. _____

_____

3. _____

_____

4. _____

_____

5. _____

_____

Words About Cultures and Customs

Locate and Use Definitions

DIRECTIONS Work with a partner. Make a vocabulary log for each word.

Example:

Word: ceremony
Definition Prediction: church service
Dictionary Definition: formal event on a special occasion
Examples: wedding, graduation, birthday
Sentence: A wedding ceremony marks the beginning of a marriage.

New Words

adjust
ceremony
culture
custom
elder
feast
privilege
respect
right
tradition

1.

Word: adjust
Definition Prediction: _____
Dictionary Definition: _____
Examples: _____
Sentence: _____

2.

Word: culture
Definition Prediction: _____
Dictionary Definition: _____
Examples: _____
Sentence: _____

3.

Word: custom
Definition Prediction: _____
Dictionary Definition: _____
Examples: _____
Sentence: _____

4.

Word: elder
Definition Prediction: _____
Dictionary Definition: _____
Examples: _____
Sentence: _____

GRAMMAR: TRANSITIVE AND INTRANSITIVE VERBS

Classical Music Meets Pop!

Vanessa-Mae Nicholson sometimes uses an electric violin.

Transitive and Intransitive Verbs

A **transitive verb** needs an object to complete its meaning. The **object** answers the question *Whom?* or *What?*

Vanessa-Mae **loves** the violin.

What does Vanessa-Mae love? The **violin**.

An **intransitive verb** does not need an object to complete its meaning.

She **plays** professionally.

DIRECTIONS Circle the verb in each sentence. Say the verb and ask *whom?* or *what?* to decide if there is an object. Underline the object if there is one. Tell if the verb is *transitive* or *intransitive*.

Type of Verb

1. Vanessa-Mae Nicholson (plays) the <u>violin</u>.   _____transitive_____

2. She travels around the world.   _____

3. She entertains in many countries.   _____

4. She thrills her fans.   _____

5. Vanessa-Mae has a Thai and Chinese heritage.   _____

6. She moved to London at the age of four.   _____

7. Her talent surprises people.   _____

8. Her concerts attract huge crowds.   _____

9. Audiences clap wildly.   _____

10. Vanessa-Mae performs classical music.   _____

11. She mixes classical and pop sounds.   _____

12. She has a style all her own.   _____

13. Her recordings sell very well.   _____

14. She wins music awards.   _____

What's Your Opinion About It?

DIRECTIONS Look back at the author's statements think about
living in two cultures. Complete the chart.

Author	Opinion	Signal Words	Do you agree? Why or Why Not?
Jenny	I think it's unfair that some people make fun of others because they have an accent.	I think	I agree. You should respect other people's feelings.
Janell			
Christian			

DIRECTIONS Write your own opinion about living in two cultures. Use signal
words, such as *think*, *feel*, *believe*, *should*, *agree*, and *disagree*.

_____

_____

_____

_____

_____

_____

_____

_____

GRAMMAR: HELPING VERBS

Could, Would, Should!

Janell's costume is decorated with fringe and beadwork.

> ### Helping Verbs
> Some verbs are made up of more than one word. The last word is the **main verb**. It shows the action. The verb that comes before it is the **helping verb**.
>
> Janell **might dance** at the powwow.

DIRECTIONS Complete each sentence with a verb from the box. Circle the helping verb.

1. Janell _____(can) do_____ some beadwork.

2. She _____ of a design first.

3. It _____ fun to see her work.

4. I wish she _____ me how to do it.

| could teach |
| can do |
| must think |
| would be |

5. Jenny _____ to read in Chinese.

6. She _____ many characters to read a Chinese newspaper.

7. She _____ a hundred characters already!

8. In the future, she _____ well in Chinese.

| must recognize |
| would like |
| might read |
| can identify |

9. Christian says we _____ at our similarities.

10. He thinks sports _____ people closer.

11. The players _____ with each other.

12. Everyone _____ a good job for the team.

| can bring |
| must communicate |
| must do |
| should look |

MORE ABOUT HELPING VERBS Look at the chart on page 99 of your book. Use helping verbs to write two sentences that tell about a possibility and two sentences that tell what someone ought to do.

© Hampton-Brown

Using a Thesaurus

DIRECTIONS Study these entries from a thesaurus.
Then answer the questions.

Thesaurus

A **thesaurus** is a book of words and their **synonyms**. Use it to find better words to express ideas. Words in a thesaurus are listed in alphabetical order.

The **entry word** is the word you look up. Next to the entry word is a list of synonyms for it.

These are the **synonyms** for the entry word. Use a dictionary to find their exact meanings.

tradesman, *n.* shopkeeper, merchant. See SALE.

tradition, *n.* belief, practice, usage, custom, culture, folklore.

traditional, *adj.* conventional, customary, formal. See CONFORMITY.

Choose a synonym for a word that is the same **part of speech**. Each synonym in this list is a noun.

This is a **reference**. Look this word up to find more synonyms and other related words.

1. What can a thesaurus help you find? _synonyms_____

2. What are the entry words? _____

3. Would you find a synonym for *trace* before or after *tradesman*? _____

4. What word can you look up to find more synonyms for *tradesman*? _____

5. How many synonyms are listed for *tradition*? _____

DIRECTIONS Choose a synonym to replace each bold word.
Check a dictionary to see if it has the exact meaning you want.

6. Dancing is a Native American _____custom_____ .
   tradition

7. I dance during cultural _____ .
   celebrations

8. I wear _____ outfits with bead designs on them.
   bright

9. The designs are made with beads of _____ colors.
   different

10. It can take months to _____ the beadwork for one outfit.
    finish

© Hampton-Brown

WRITING: A SELF-PORTRAIT

The One and Only You

DIRECTIONS Write a self-portrait. Include a drawing or photo of yourself. If you are using a word-processing program, see Handbook pages 383–389 for help.

A Self-Portrait

A **self-portrait** describes who you are and what you are like. It tells about your experiences and how you feel about them.

Tell who you are, where you are from, and what you like to do.

_____

_____

_____

_____

_____

_____

Tell about a tradition or custom that makes your culture special.

_____

_____

_____

_____

_____

_____

Express your opinions about living in two cultures. Tell what you think and how you feel. Explain how it is difficult or easy.

_____

_____

_____

_____

_____

_____

He Loved the Game!

Roberto Clemente loved helping people in need. As a baseball player and as a humanitarian, he helped "bridge the gap."

> ### Pronouns
>
> A **pronoun** takes the place of a noun. The noun is called the **antecedent**.
>
> <u>Clemente</u> played baseball. **He** was a pitcher.
> antecedent   pronoun
>
> Some pronouns can be the subject of a sentence. Other pronouns show who owns something.
>
> **He** loved baseball, and **he** loved people. Helping others was one of **his** values.

DIRECTIONS Work with a partner. Read about Roberto Clemente. Look at the underlined antecedent. Write the correct pronoun.

1. <u>Roberto Clemente</u> was born in Puerto Rico in 1934. _____His_____ family was poor.

2. <u>Roberto</u> loved baseball. _____ wanted to play in the pros.

3. <u>Baseball scouts</u> watched Roberto. They wanted him on _____ teams.

4. <u>Roberto</u> missed the country of his birth when _____ went to the United States.

5. Roberto played for a team in <u>Pittsburgh</u>. The city was proud of _____ talented player.

6. The Pittsburgh <u>fans</u> loved Roberto Clemente. _____ thought he was a great athlete.

7. His throwing <u>arm</u> was fast. _____ was like a cannon.

8. <u>Roberto</u> once said, "_____ was born to play baseball."

9. In 1964, Roberto married a Puerto Rican <u>woman</u>. _____ name was Vera Zabala.

10. In 1972, <u>Roberto and several others</u> died in a plane crash. _____ were on their way to help earthquake victims in Nicaragua.

11. <u>Vera</u> was left alone with three sons. _____ shared her loss with a nation in mourning.

12. A year after _____ death, <u>Roberto</u> was elected to the National Baseball Hall of Fame.

Subject Pronouns	
I	we
you	they
she	
he	
it	

Pronouns That Show Who Owns Something	
my	our
your	their
her	
his	
its	

Words About Conflict

New Words

- abuse
- challenge
- compete
- cruel
- hostility
- humiliation
- intimidate
- petition
- racial prejudice
- threat

Use Context Clues

DIRECTIONS Read the paragraph. Replace each bold word with the correct new word.

In the 1940s, black baseball players were allowed to join white players on

Major League teams. Still, black players had to live with a lot of

___hostility / abuse___ from fans and other players. Some
1. hateful actions

tried to _____ them. Much of the
2. scare

_____ did hurt the black players. But by the
3. mean treatment

1950s, blacks and whites began to _____
4. take a stand against

this treatment. They thought blacks should be able to

_____ in sports and other jobs. Some even sent a
5. try to win

_____ to the government. In the United States many
6. form that asks for change

people are still working to stop _____.
7. bad feelings toward people because of their race

Satchel Paige was not allowed to play in the Major Leagues for many years.

Use New Words in Context

DIRECTIONS Write a sentence for each word.

8. cruel: _____

_____

9. humiliation: _____

_____

10. threat: _____

_____

LITERARY ANALYSIS: NARRATOR'S POINT OF VIEW

Look Who's Talking

DIRECTIONS Rewrite each paragraph. Change the point of view.

1. First-Person Point of View:

I was very excited. My basketball team was playing in the state championship. I was tying my shoes when Coach West came up to me.

"I want you to start the game today, Catherine," said Coach West.

I couldn't believe my ears! To start a game was my dream come true.

Third-Person Point of View:

_____

_____

_____

_____

2. Third-Person Point of View:

Enrique loves his grandmother's visits because his father makes a special meal for her. Papi lets Enrique and his sisters help. Enrique stirs the barbecue sauce. His sisters set the table. His family gathers for a wonderful meal. Enrique eats his favorite foods with his favorite people.

First-Person Point of View:

_____

_____

_____

_____

_____

_____

© Hampton-Brown

Connecting What You Know

DIRECTIONS Follow the steps to connect new information to what you know.

1 **Preview the Article** Read the title. Then look at the picture and read the caption.

2 **Start a K-W-L Chart** Write what you know about Wilma in the "K" column. Write what you want to learn in the "W" column.

Wilma Rudolph, Runner

Wilma Rudolph was born in Tennessee in 1940. She was often very ill as a young child. Wilma had polio, double pneumonia, and scarlet fever. She could not walk normally until she was 11 years old.

Wilma did not let illness stop her. She worked hard to make her weak leg strong. By the time Wilma reached high school, she was able to play basketball. Her life as an athlete had begun!

Wilma competed in the 1956 Olympic Games in Melbourne, Australia. She was a member of the relay team that won a bronze medal.

In the 1960 Olympics in Rome, Italy, Wilma competed in three events. She ran in the 100-meter dash, the 200-meter dash, and the 4 x 100-meter relay.

She was the first American woman to win three gold medals in a single Olympic Games.

Wilma Rudolph crosses the finish line in Rome.

3 **Tell What You Learned** Read the article. Then complete the "L" column.

K-W-L Chart

K What I Know	W What I Want to Learn	L What I Learned

GRAMMAR: PRONOUN AGREEMENT

Soccer Sentences

Pronouns

A **pronoun** takes the place of a noun. The noun that it replaces is called its **antecedent**.

María Delgado is an athlete. **She** plays soccer.
    antecedent   pronoun

The pronoun must agree in type and number with its antecedent.

Deacon can pick up the ball. ~~They~~ plays goalie.
                                          He
                                          ^

Start

Ramón and Jenna play on a team. _____ team's name is the Eagles.

The Bruins are the champs. "_____ team is the best!" they chant.

María plays fullback. She says, "Soccer is _____ favorite sport."

Toshiro puts a ball on the field. He kicks _____ into the air.

The Hotshots like their flag. _____ design is fantastic!

How to Play
Soccer Sentences

1. Play in a group of three. One person is the "referee." The others are the players.

2. Each player places a small object on START and then uses a coin to move:

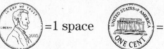 =1 space    =2 spaces

3. A player reads the sentences and adds the correct pronoun.

   Example: Mia kicks the ball.
   ___It___ whizzes past.

4. The "referee" decides if the answer is correct. A player scores 1 goal for each correct answer.

5. The game ends when one player gets 10 goals.

Deacon asks Chi, "Do _____ want to play forward?"

The coach warms up her players. She has _____ do sit-ups.

An older girl is referee. _____ calls time-out.

Bo kicks the ball to Carlos. Carlos knocks it back with _____ head.

Coretta wants to play goalie. "Can _____ play goalie?" she asks.

Using an Almanac

DIRECTIONS Study the index and the article from an almanac. Answer the questions.

Almanac

An **almanac** is a reference book that gives facts about a wide range of topics. It has tables, lists, diagrams, and special features that provide information. Almanacs are updated each year.

INDEX

Soccer, 239
Soil erosion, 73
Solar eclipse, 186
Solar system
  exploration of, 185
  facts about, 182–184
Solomon islands, 154–155

PLANETS, STARS, AND SPACE TRAVEL

EXPLORING the SOLAR SYSTEM

American space exploration began in January 1958, when the Explorer I satellite was launched into orbit. In 1958, NASA (The National Aeronautics and Space Administration) was formed. To the right are some unmanned space missions launched by NASA.

The Search for LIFE BEYOND EARTH

For years scientists have tried to discover if there is life on other planets in our solar system or elsewhere. They look for signs of what is needed for life on Earth—basics like water and proper temperature.

WHAT SCIENTISTS HAVE LEARNED

Mars and Jupiter. In 1996, two teams of scientists examined two meteorites that may have come from **Mars** and found evidence that some form of life may have existed on Mars billions of years ago. In 1997 and 1998, photographs of Europa, a moon of **Jupiter**, showed areas of water. Europa may have had an ocean

1962–Mariner 2
First successful flyby of Venus.

1964–Mariner 4
First probe to reach Mars, 1965.

1972–Pioneer 10
First probe to reach Jupiter, 1973.

1973–Mariner 10
Only U.S. probe to Mercury, 1974.

1975–Viking 1 and 2
Landed on Mars in 1976.

1977–Voyager 1
Reached Jupiter in 1979 and Saturn in 1980.

1977–Voyager 2
Reached Jupiter in 1979, Saturn in 1981, Uranus in 1986, Neptune in 1989.

1978–Pioneer Venus 1
Operated in Venus orbit 14 years.

1989–Magellan

1. On which page can you find out what a solar eclipse is? _186_____

2. On which page would you find the article shown above? _____

3. Under which heading in the article can you find out about space exploration?

   _____

4. What does the feature to the right of the article show? _____

   _____

5. Skim the last paragraph. What evidence did meteorites provide about Mars? _____

   _____

6. Would you use this article for a research report about NASA? Why or why not? _____

   _____

   _____

Name _____ Date _____

Investigate Media

DIRECTIONS Use this planner to help you investigate how one type of media reports an event. Discuss your findings with groups that studied the other types of media.

Group members : _____

Type of media to research: ☐ TV and videos ☐ radio ☐ newspaper and other print

Our Notes

Name and date of the event: _____

Name of the program or printed material: _____

Kinds of Information Given	Visuals	Evaluation
☐ facts ☐ sound bites ☐ quotes ☐ background	Describe any graphics, photos, or video clips.	It was effective/not effective because
Quality Checklist	_____	_____
☐ Helpful background information is given.	_____	_____
☐ The report answers the questions *Who? What? Where? When? Why?* and *How?*	_____	_____
☐ Enough facts and details are provided.	_____	_____
☐ Visuals add useful information.	_____	_____
☐ No opinions are expressed.	_____	_____
☐ The report can be clearly understood.	_____	_____

Community Words

New Words

benefit
community
conversation
excuse
harvest festival
provide
recognize
trade

Define Words

DIRECTIONS Write a definition for each new word.
Use your own words.

1. benefit: _something good_____

2. trade: _____

3. harvest festival: _____

4. conversation: _____

5. provide: _____

6. recognize: _____

7. excuse: _____

8. community: _____

Use New Words in Context

DIRECTIONS Draw a line to match the beginning of
each sentence with its ending.

9. Everyone in my **community**   to eat, dance, and sing.

10. The garden **provides**   with friends about the garden.

11. After the growing season   a place for neighbors to meet.

12. My friends **recognize**   works in the city garden.

13. We **trade** vegetables   me even though I cut my hair.

14. The festival is a good **excuse**   we have a **harvest festival**.

15. We have **conversations**   a **benefit** of having a garden.

16. Good, fresh food is   for fruit.

GRAMMAR: POSSESSIVE NOUNS AND PRONOUNS

A Garden of Possessives

DIRECTIONS Rewrite each sentence. Use a possessive noun to replace the underlined words. Look on Handbook page 436 for help with forming possessive nouns.

> ### Possessive Nouns and Pronouns
>
> A **possessive noun** shows who owns or has something. Possessive nouns have an apostrophe.
>
> > **Royce's** garden (the garden belonging to Royce)
> > the **girls'** shovels (the shovels the girls have)
>
> A **possessive pronoun** also tells who owns or has something.
>
> > **Their** garden is beautiful.
> > I'm proud of **mine** too.

1. The <u>garden planted by Amir</u> has eggplants and other vegetables. _____

   Amir's garden has eggplants and other vegetables.

2. The pale, purple color <u>that the eggplant has</u> is strange. _____

   _____

3. The Italian lady admires the plants <u>belonging to her neighbor.</u> _____

   _____

4. The gardens <u>grown by the friends</u> have lovely flowers. _____

   _____

5. The festival <u>of the gardeners</u> is a happy event. _____

   _____

DIRECTIONS Choose a pronoun from the box to complete each sentence.

6. This is the neighbors' garden. It is _____*theirs*_____ .

7. This is the Polish man's space. It is _____ .

8. This is the street you and I live on. It is _____ street.

9. This is the apartment where I live. It is _____ .

10. This is the Indian woman's basket. It is _____ basket.

my	mine
your	yours
her	hers
his	his
our	ours
their	theirs

A Sequence of Garden Events

DIRECTIONS Read the story events on page 124 of your book.
Finish the time line.

1980

1. _____

   _____

1981

2. _____

1982

3. Amir started working in the garden. _____

4. _____

5. _____

6. _____

DIRECTIONS Think about changes the garden caused. Answer the questions.

7. How did the garden change the way Amir looks at people?

_____

_____

8. How did the garden change the ways other people in the community
feel about each other?

_____

_____

Starting from Scratch!

DIRECTIONS Work with a partner. Complete the article with words from the box.

_____Everybody_____ loves to see a bright, pretty
          1.

garden. Thanks to a woman named Liz Christy, New

York City is dotted with _____many_____ of these green wonderlands.
                          2.

After I read about Ms. Christy, I looked around my city. _____ of
                                                              3.

our neighborhoods had trash-cluttered lots. _____ were right near
                                              4.

my house. I presented an idea for cleaning up the lots to my schoolmates. Now

_____ wants to help.
      5.

Volunteers work together every weekend. A _____ come early
                                            6.

every Saturday morning. _____ of the volunteers does something.
                          7.

_____ clear away trash. _____ help to plant.
      8.   **9.**

Businesses help, too. _____ donate seeds and plants.
                        10.

_____ works together.
      11.

We have already planted two community gardens! _____
                                                  12.

provides food and a peaceful space. One garden grows berries; the other grows

vegetables. _____ provide beauty.
              13.

_____ has changed in our city. _____ can see it!
      14.   **15.**

Indefinite Pronouns
When you are not talking about a specific person or thing, use an **indefinite pronoun**.
Everyone is working in the garden.
Singular indefinite pronouns need a singular verb.
Each of the neighbors **has** a garden plot.
Plural indefinite pronouns need a plural verb.
A **few** of the gardens **have** scarecrows.

Singular Indefinite Pronouns
somebody
everybody
everyone
anyone
nobody
no one
each
anything
something
nothing
some
all

Plural Indefinite Pronouns
many
several
both
few
some
all

MORE ABOUT INDEFINITE PRONOUNS List the indefinite pronouns that you did not use. Use each one as the subject of a sentence. Make sure the verb agrees with the subject.

A Different Point of View

DIRECTIONS Retell an event from "Amir." Use a different character's point of view.

1 **Choose an Event** List details that describe the event. You might want to use a cluster like the one on Handbook page 370.

2 **Choose a Character** What did your character hear, see, or do during the event? How did your character feel about what happened?

3 **Write the Story** Tell about the event from your character's point of view. For help with the **writing process**, see Handbook pages 408–413.

Point of View

A story's **point of view** is the position or angle from which the story is told. In "Amir," the reader finds out how Amir thinks and feels because the author tells the story from that character's point of view.

Title: _____

Beginning
Tell about the setting and action. Tell what your character wanted or what problem your character had. Use the pronouns *I*, *me*, and *my* to show your character's point of view.

_____
_____
_____
_____
_____

Middle
Use lots of details to describe the event. Express your character's feelings about what happened.

_____
_____
_____
_____
_____
_____

Conclusion
Tell how the problem was resolved. How did your character feel at the end of the event?

_____
_____
_____

4 **Read the Story Aloud** See if your classmates can identify whose point of view you have described.

Research Food Chains

DIRECTIONS Follow the steps to research a food chain.

1 Write the environment or habitat that you will study.

2 Research what the animals in the environment eat. Take notes on separate paper.

3 Review your notes. Look for plants and animals that form a food chain. Then complete the diagram. Use pictures or words. Start at the bottom.

Food Chain for: _____

4 Decide how to present your information. What will you show? Tell how it will help to explain the information. See Handbook pages 390-391 for tips.

☐ poster ☐ diorama ☐ computer graphics ☐ video ☐ recordings of nature sounds

_____

_____

5 Prepare your visuals, models, or recordings. Then practice your presentation. Share the information with your class.

Words for Planning a Garden

New Words

fee

imagine

information

interested

local

lot

owner

permission

steer

Use New Words in Context

DIRECTIONS Read each sentence. Rewrite the sentence.
Replace each bold word with a new word.

1. In my mind, I could **see** a beautiful garden.

   _____

2. My friends made a community garden on that **small piece of land**.

   _____

3. Mr. Garcia, **the man who owns the land**, gave his **approval**.

   _____

4. He said there would be no **money charged** for using the land.

   _____

5. The **neighborhood** newspaper printed **facts** about our garden.

   _____

6. **Caring** people in the community got involved.

   _____

7. I can **guide** you toward resources you will need to plant a garden.

   _____

8. You can find many garden supplies in a **close to home** hardware store.

   _____

Neighbors work together in a community garden.

MORE ABOUT GARDEN WORDS Pretend that your club is planning a
car wash. Use new words to tell how you would plan the event.
Share your plan with a partner.

GRAMMAR: PROGRESSIVE FORMS OF VERBS

A Garden Is Emerging!

Progressive Forms of Verbs

The **present progressive** form of a verb tells about an action as it is happening. It uses the helping verb **am**, **is**, or **are** plus a **present participle**.

Today, she **is planting** the seeds.

The **past progressive** form tells about an action that happened over time in the past. It uses the helping verb **was** or **were** plus a **present participle**.

Yesterday, she **was preparing** the soil.

DIRECTIONS Complete each sentence. Use the present progressive form of the verb in parentheses.

1. Today, I _____*am digging*_____ a garden. (**dig**)

2. My father _____ with me. (**work**)

3. We _____ lettuce, beans, and peas. (**plant**)

4. My father _____ a trellis for the beans to climb. (**build**)

5. I _____ holes for bean and pea seeds. (**make**)

6. We _____ lettuce from a friend's garden. (**transplant**)

DIRECTIONS Complete each sentence. Use the past progressive form of the verb in parentheses.

7. Last week, Dad and I _____ our crops. (**tend**)

8. We _____ the day when we could harvest something. (**anticipate**)

9. I _____ for bugs hidden in the vines. (**search**)

10. I _____ under a leaf, and there they were! (**look**)

11. Pea pods _____ out all over. (**pop**)

12. At last, our garden _____ food for our winter meals. (**produce**)

© Hampton-Brown

What's Important?

DIRECTIONS Decide what information is important before starting a community garden.

1 Review the List of Things to Do on page 130. You might want to add other things to do.

_____

_____

_____

2 Then finish the T-chart. Answer the questions.

- To plan a garden, is it important to know the address?   _____

- Do you need gardening shoes and hats to plan the garden?   _____

- Do you need to name the garden to plan it?   _____

Important Things	Unimportant Things
Find out who the owner is.	

3 Compare your T-chart with a partner's. Discuss the differences. Do you want to change yours?

4 With your partner, explain your chart to other students. Tell why each important thing must be done before you start your garden.

Compare Country and City Gardens

DIRECTIONS Work in a team of four. Two students can research city gardens and two can research country gardens.

1 Gather information with your partner. Then fill in your part of the chart.

Research Questions	City Garden	Country Garden
What plants grow best in this area?		
What insects or animals are found here? How do they affect the plants?		
Should pesticides be used? Why or why not?		
How can the plants be protected?		
How does pollution affect the plants?		

2 Meet with your team to compare and discuss your charts.

3 Name the three most important considerations for planting each kind of garden.

- For a city garden, consider _____

  _____

  _____ .

- For a country garden, consider _____

  _____

  _____ .

© Hampton-Brown

Name _____   Date _____

Dreams and Decisions

DIRECTIONS Use the mind map to write about your own dreams and decisions. Tell about other dreams and decisions as you read the selections in this unit.

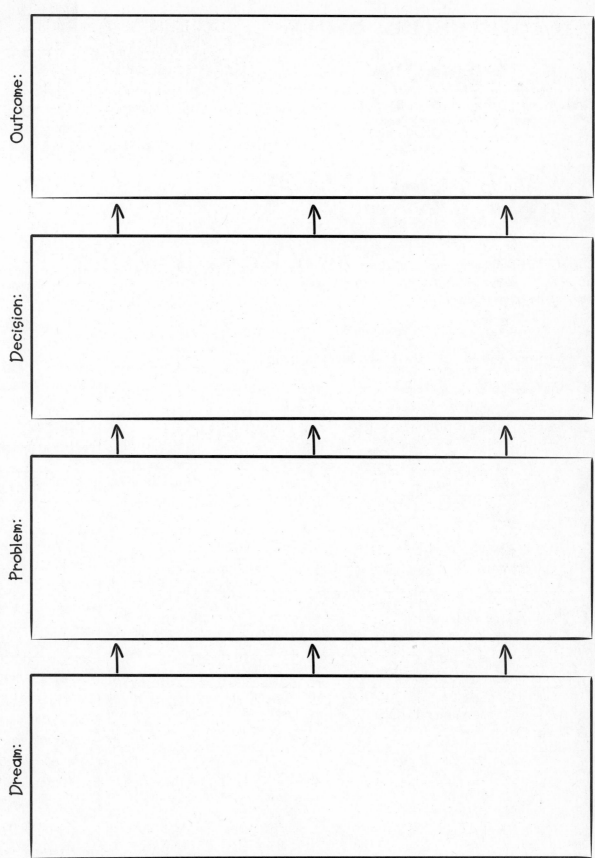

Outcome:

Decision:

Problem:

Dream:

An Interesting Story

Vietnamese potbellied pigs grow to about 100 pounds in weight. They live to between 12 and 17 years of age.

Adding Details to Sentences

There are many ways to add details to sentences.

Use an **adjective** to describe a noun or pronoun.

The **potbellied** pig has **white** fur.

Use an **adverb** to tell how, where, or when.

The pig looks up **eagerly**.

Use a **prepositional phrase** to add details like where, when, or for what purpose.

My friend adopts the pig **as a pet**.

DIRECTIONS Rewrite each sentence. Make it more interesting. Add adjectives, adverbs, and prepositional phrases from the boxes, or add some of your own.

1. My friend Tan adopted a Vietnamese potbellied pig.

   My good friend Tan generously adopted a spotted

   Vietnamese potbellied pig.

2. One day, Tan's pig noticed a smell.

   _____

   _____

3. The pig dug.

   _____

   _____

4. The sofa was destroyed.

   _____

   _____

5. Tan says, "I recommend you learn about pigs."

   _____

   _____

Adjectives	
tasty	potbellied
lovely	hungry
good	domestic
pudgy	beautiful
naughty	spotted
delicious	wonderful

Adverbs	
busily	strongly
quickly	generously
inside	almost
nearly	always

Prepositional Phrases
with his nose
for a treat
before adopting one
within seconds
under the sofa
in the living room
beneath a pillow
in two minutes

Words About Chinese Immigrants

New Words

- craftsmanship
- debt
- epidemic
- garment
- ginger root
- gold field
- merchant
- miner
- tailor
- tower

Relate Words

DIRECTIONS Write the new words where they belong.

People	Places	Things

Use New Words in Context

DIRECTIONS Write the new words to finish the paragraph.

In 1849, gold fever spread like an _____epidemic_____ around the
1.

world. Chinese immigrants and many others rushed to California. They worked as

_____ in the gold fields. Some of them had to repay huge
2.

_____ when they arrived. In their dreams, they saw gold coins
3.

stacked as high as a _____ . Some of the new immigrants did not
4.

become miners, however. _____ opened stores and sold goods.
5.

Tailors used their _____ to sew _____ .
6.   7.

Importers sold favorite spices, such as _____ .
8.

MORE ABOUT NEW WORDS Work with a partner. Give definitions for the new
words, one at a time. Have your partner say the word that matches
each definition.

Description

DIRECTIONS Read the description. Use the sensory words to visualize the fabric. Then complete the chart.

> **Description**
>
> A **description** gives a clear picture of a person, place, or thing. It has **sensory words** that appeal to the five senses. This helps the reader **visualize** the scene.

> Yadira touched the smooth, silky fabric. It was the color of a glowing sunset, and whispered like a gentle breeze when it moved. The folds caressed her arms like firelight. Her scissors slipped through the cloth like a silvery ship on a coral sea.

Sensory Words	Visualization	Senses Used
smooth, silky	soft, shiny	touch, sight

DIRECTIONS Choose a school activity, a place, or a favorite meal to describe. Brainstorm sensory words for your topic. Then write a description.

Scene: _____

Sensory Words	Description
Sight:	
Sound:	
Touch:	
Smell:	
Taste:	

Speak Up

DIRECTIONS Read the story all the way through. Then look at the underlined dialogue and complete the chart.

Story	What the Dialogue Shows About the Character
1. The boy frowned. "Why do you have to go away?"	This shows that the boy is unhappy and wants someone to explain.
2. "You don't understand me at all!" cried Marnie.	This shows that _____ _____ _____ .
3. "I understand that you think you are too good for our little town," responded the boy.	This shows that _____ _____ _____ .
4. "That's not true! But if I don't see what the world is like, how can I know who I really am?" Marnie cried.	This shows that _____ _____ _____ .
5. Then, seeing the boy's face, she whispered, "I don't want to leave you, but I have to see some of the world."	This shows that _____ _____ _____ .
6. "Okay," sighed the boy. "Go explore the world and when you return, I'll be waiting for you."	This shows that _____ _____ _____ .

> **Dialogue**
>
> **Dialogue** is what characters say to each other. It can show what the characters are like and explain their actions.
>
> Most dialogue is set off by quotation marks.
>
> "I don't want to leave you, but I have to see some of the world," Marnie explained.

MORE ABOUT DIALOGUE Write a short dialogue for two characters. Have a partner read the dialogue and tell you what it shows about the characters.

New Outcomes

DIRECTIONS Work with a partner. Study the different actions the characters could have taken. How would each different action affect the outcome?

Different Actions	New Outcomes
1. Yenna falls in love with one of her suitors while the young man is gone.	She marries the wealthy suitor and becomes a grand lady of leisure. She has many children and grandchildren. The young man never sees her again.
2. The young man marries someone else at the gold fields. Yenna waits for him in San Francisco.	
3. The young man never returns to San Francisco. After two years, Yenna decides not to wait for him any longer.	
4. Yenna leaves her father and goes with the young man to his farm.	
5. The young man refuses to live with Yenna and her father.	

DIRECTIONS Choose a new outcome from your chart and circle it. Then write a new story ending.

What the characters say:	What the characters do:
_____	_____
_____	_____
_____	_____
_____	_____
_____	_____

Historic Letters

DIRECTIONS Work with a small group. Read the article. Circle the adjectives. Write each adjective in the correct column of the chart.

In 1850, a boat sailed into the (crowded) harbor in San Francisco. On the boat were Louise Clappe, her husband, and her two sisters. They had come all the way from (central) Massachusetts. Leaving his wife in San Francisco, Dr. Fayette Clappe traveled to a rough camp in the Sierras to open a medical practice. Eventually, Louise joined him.

Over fifteen months, Louise wrote twenty-three letters from the camps. Her first letter describes her wild journey to the camp. The letters describe a distant time in American history. They tell about the French and Spanish miners and people from around the world. They describe the steep mountains, the brilliant river, and the crude buildings.

Louise wrote her last letter in November, 1852. After that, she returned to San Francisco and taught school for twenty-four years. She died in New Jersey in 1906.

Adjectives

An **adjective** describes a noun or pronoun. Adjectives can tell how many, how much, which one, or what something is like.

> The **second** letter describes the **important** rooms in the **grand** Empire Hotel.

A **proper adjective** comes from a proper noun.

> The letters bring **American** history to life.

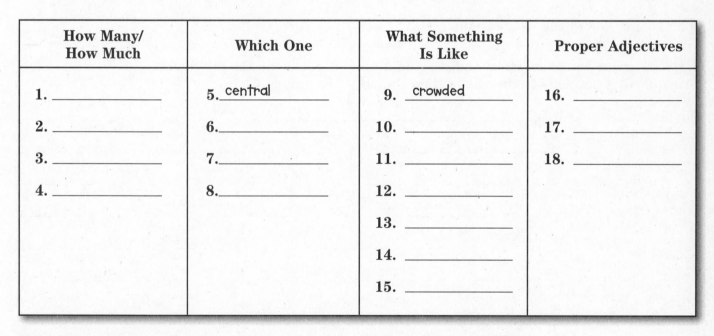

How Many/ How Much	Which One	What Something Is Like	Proper Adjectives
1. _____	5. central	9. crowded	16. _____
2. _____	6. _____	10. _____	17. _____
3. _____	7. _____	11. _____	18. _____
4. _____	8. _____	12. _____	
		13. _____	
		14. _____	
		15. _____	

MORE ABOUT ADJECTIVES Work with your group to add sparkle to the passage. Replace six adjectives with more descriptive ones. Use the proofreading marks on Handbook page 412 to make changes.

WRITING: A STORY OUTCOME

A Different Ending

Nights passed into weeks, months turned into years . . .

DIRECTIONS Work with a partner. Follow the steps to write a new ending for "Ginger for the Heart."

1 Brainstorm how the new goals and actions could affect the story's outcome. Write a new outcome for each new action.

Character	New Goal	New Actions	New Outcome
Yenna	She wants to please the young man.	When the young man returns, Yenna leaves her father.	
the young man	He wants to get rich.	The young man stays in the gold fields. He never returns to Yenna.	

2 Choose one of the new outcomes.

3 Now write your new story ending. Add details to describe the outcome. Tell what happens to the characters. Include dialogue.

_____

_____

_____

_____

_____

_____

_____

_____

_____

4 Read your work in a group. Discuss how the new goals and actions led to the new outcomes.

RESEARCH SKILLS

Using a Map

DIRECTIONS Study the map. Then follow the steps to give your partner directions to a place.

San Francisco Bay Area

The **compass rose** shows which directions are north, south, east, and west on the map.

The **scale** shows how to measure distances on a map. On this map, one inch equals 36 miles.

1. Write three cities and three destinations in the chart. Then write the directions from each city to a destination.

2. Cover up or erase the destinations. Then trade charts with your partner.

3. Have your partner read the directions and use the map to figure out the destinations.

Starting Point	Destination	Directions
Merced	Modesto	Go west 20 miles, then go north 24 miles.

Compare Travel Rates

DIRECTIONS Calculate and compare rates of travel.

1 Calculate the different rates of travel for a trip from Omaha, Nebraska, to Sacramento, California. Complete the data grid.

Omaha is in Nebraska, near the center of the United States. Sacramento is near the Pacific coast in California.

Formula: $\dfrac{\text{distance}}{\text{time}} = \text{rate}$

Trip	Means of Travel	Distance	Approximate Time	Rate
Omaha to Sacramento	car	1,588 miles	50 hours	
	train	1,853 miles	41.5 hours	
	plane	1,370 miles	4.5 hours	

2 Use the formula to find out how many times faster it is to travel by train than by car. Then use it to calculate how many times faster it is by plane than by train.

Formula: $\dfrac{\text{rate by train}}{\text{rate by car}} = \text{X times faster by train}$

• It is _____ times faster to travel by train than by car.

• It is _____ times faster to travel by plane than by train.

3 Which means of travel would you use to go from Omaha to Sacramento? Why? Discuss your answer with a partner or a group.

_____

_____

_____

_____

_____

_____

Words That Matter

Use New Words in Context

DIRECTIONS Choose another new word that goes with each word.
Use each pair in a sentence.

New Words

advanced
condition
confident
determined
excel
extraordinary
hearing–impaired
independent
opportunity
secure

Words That Go Together	Sentences
advanced hearing–impaired	There are many advanced techniques to help hearing–impaired people.
excel _____	
confident _____	
independent _____	
condition _____	

Identify Antonyms

DIRECTIONS Write an antonym for each new word in the chart.
Use a thesaurus if you need to.

New Word	Antonym
extraordinary	ordinary
secure	_____
advanced	_____
confident	_____
independent	_____

Double Up!

Neshmayda and Suzette were born deaf and use sign language to communicate.

> ## Compound Predicates
> A **compound predicate** has two or more verbs joined by the conjunction **and** or **or**. Both verbs agree with the subject.
>
> The Aguayos **hear** about a school **and enroll** the twins.

DIRECTIONS Underline the two verbs in each sentence. Circle the conjunction. Draw an arrow from the subject to each verb.

1. The twins live in their own world (and) experience life as one person.

2. They watch other children or play by themselves.

3. To communicate with each other, the girls point or make noises.

4. Later, the Aguayos discover the girls' deafness and wonder what to do.

5. They move to Washington, D.C., and enroll the twins in the Gallaudet school for the deaf.

6. The Aguayos learn sign language and communicate with Neshy and Suzy.

DIRECTIONS Proofread each sentence. Use the Proofreading Marks on Handbook page 412 to make any necessary corrections.

7. As toddlers, the twins looks the same and acts the same.

8. They plays and communicate in special ways.

9. At first, their parents do not notice or diagnose their daughters' hearing problems.

10. Later, the Aguayos learn sign language and communicates with the girls.

11. Suzy talk to her mother and tell about a hospital visit.

12. Mrs. Aguayo learns about the twins' experiences and cry.

© Hampton-Brown

A Happy Occasion

DIRECTIONS Work with a partner. Think about weddings you have attended or seen on television. Complete the sentences. Write a compound subject using *and* or *or*. Make sure your compound subject agrees with the verb.

1. _Weddings and anniversaries_____ are happy occasions.

2. _____ dress up for the wedding.

3. Either _____ cover the heads of many brides.

4. _____ carry bouquets of fresh flowers.

5. _____ makes the room glow.

6. Either _____ play music for the bride and groom.

7. _____ is a nice place for a wedding reception.

8. Either _____ brings in the wedding cake.

9. _____ cut the cake.

10. _____ serve cake to the guests.

11. _____ give gifts and best wishes.

12. _____ helps people remember the wedding.

Suzette and Neshmayda had a double wedding ceremony in 1999. The ceremony was conducted in speaking and signing.

Paraphrase and Compare Literature

DIRECTIONS What matters most to the people in "Twins"? Paraphrase information from the selection to complete the chart.

The Aguayo Family	What Matters Most?	How Do You Know?
Maria and Joaquin Aguayo		
Neshy and Suzy Aguayo		

DIRECTIONS Compare "Twins" to another selection. Choose one idea. Write three paragraphs.

☐ I will compare **Yenna** from "Ginger for the Heart" with **Neshy and Suzy** from "Twins."

☐ I will compare the **essay** "Talking Walls" with the **article** "Twins."

☐ I will compare the **problems and solutions** in "Teammates" with those in "Twins."

Paragraph 1:
How are the two selections alike?

_____

_____

_____

Paragraph 2:
How are the two selections different?

_____

_____

_____

Paragraph 3:
Which selection is your favorite? What makes the strongest impression on you?

_____

_____

_____

_____

GRAMMAR: ADJECTIVES THAT COMPARE

Family Comparisons

Whitewater rafting is a thrilling adventure for many.

> ### Adjectives That Compare
>
> A **comparative adjective** compares two things.
>> My sister is **quieter** than I am.
>> She is **less sociable** than me, too.
>
> A **superlative adjective** compares three or more things.
>> I am the **friendliest** person in the family.
>> I am the **most sociable** person in my home!
>
> Use **–er** and **–est** for most two-syllable adjectives. Use **less / more** and **least / most** for words with three or more syllables.

DIRECTIONS Complete each sentence. Write the correct form of the adjective in parentheses.

1. Jayesh is _____*more adventurous*_____ than his twin brother, Kuval. (**adventurous**)

2. He wants to raft down the _____ river in the West. (**wild**)

3. He wants to climb the _____ peak on the continent. (**high**)

4. Jayesh is _____ than Kuval. (**studious**)

5. Kuval is _____ than his brother. (**calm**)

6. To Kuval, drawing is the _____ thing in the world! (**exciting**)

DIRECTIONS Write sentences to compare people you know. Use the correct forms of the adjectives in the box or some of your own.

7. _*My sister is less confident than I am.*_____

8. _____

9. _____

10. _____

11. _____

12. _____

| creative |
| independent |
| tidy |
| nice |
| confident |
| funny |
| strong |
| athletic |
| musical |
| young |
| serious |
| friendly |

© Hampton-Brown

Research Twins

A twin always has a friend to lean on.

DIRECTIONS Follow the steps to research twins with your group.

1 **What do you want to find out about twins? Brainstorm a list of research questions.**

Our group's questions are: _____

_____

_____

_____

2 **Decide who will research the answer for each question.**

My question to research is: _____

3 **Find information. List your sources.**

☐ books   ☐ Web sites   ☐ other

_____   _____   _____

_____   _____   _____

4 **Take notes. Write your research question and the answer you find.**

Fact Sheet About Twins

Question	Answer

5 **Share your notes with the rest of your group. Add them to a group fact sheet. Share your group's findings with the class.**

BUILD LANGUAGE AND VOCABULARY

A Detailed Description

The Oregon Trail, Albert Bierstadt, oil on canvas, Copyright © 1869

The pioneers encountered many hardships as they traveled west on the Oregon Trail. They also saw great beauty.

Complex Sentences

A **complex sentence** has one independent clause and one or more dependent clauses.

An independent clause can stand alone as a sentence. The dependent clause often begins with a **subordinating conjunction**.

The pioneers will start new lives
independent clause
when they reach Oregon.
dependent clause

DIRECTIONS Read each sentence. Underline the independent clause. Circle the dependent clause. Then write the subordinating conjunction.

1. (When night falls,) the pioneers make camp. _____When_____

2. They stop where it is safe and sheltered. _____

3. They will sleep under the stars unless it rains. _____

4. The oxen rest while the weary travelers unpack. _____

5. The night is not dark because the moon is full. _____

6. If clouds cover the moon, the sky will be black. _____

7. One man gathers wood while another carries a bucket of water. _____

8. The children help since there is much to do. _____

9. They might play simple games if they finish their chores. _____

10. Although the air is cold, the travelers stay warm by the fire. _____

11. Since the river is calm, the women wash clothes. _____

12. The pioneers carry few possessions because their wagons are small. _____

13. When the work is done, the travelers bed down for the night. _____

14. The travelers will sleep fitfully until morning breaks. _____

15. Although they have a long way to go, the pioneers will make it. _____

People on the Move

New Words

adversity

exodus

migration

newcomer

population shift

replace

segregation

shortage

triumph

Paraphrase Definitions

DIRECTIONS Use your own words to define the new words.

1. population shift _____

_____

_____

2. segregation _____

_____

_____

3. shortage _____

_____

_____

4. adversity _____

_____

_____

5. migration _____

_____

_____

Relate Words

DIRECTIONS Work with a group. Use the new words to complete the word map.

What is it?
The <u>migration</u> of people from one place to another.

Word: exodus

What are some reasons for it?

What happens?

© Hampton-Brown

If You Were an Artist . . .

DIRECTIONS Finish each sentence. Write a dependent clause using *if* or an independent clause using *then*.

> ### Complex Sentences
>
> A **complex sentence** has one independent clause and one or more dependent clauses. In some complex sentences, **if** introduces the dependent clause and **then** introduces the independent clause.
>
> **If** I like the painting, **then** I will buy it.
> <u>dependent clause</u>   <u>independent clause</u>

1. _If you take art lessons_ _____ , then you will learn how to paint.

2. If you want to paint well, _____ .

3. If you want to paint like Jacob Lawrence, _____

   _____ .

4. If Jacob Lawrence was your teacher, _____

   _____ .

5. _____ , then they can paint with you.

6. _____ , then you can turn it into a studio.

7. If you use bright colors, _____

   _____ .

8. If you use soft blues and greens, _____

   _____ .

9. _____

   _____ , then you should paint outside.

10. _____

    _____ , then you will have a self-portrait.

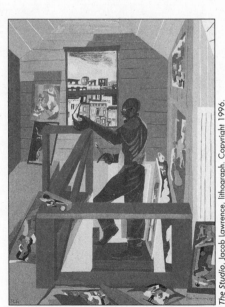

This self-portrait shows Jacob Lawrence in his studio.

The Studio, Jacob Lawrence, lithograph. Copyright 1996.

All Aboard!

DIRECTIONS Underline the prepositional phrase or phrases in each sentence. Circle the preposition. If you need help, see Handbook page 456.

> ### Prepositional Phrases
> A **prepositional phrase** starts with a **preposition** and ends with a noun or a pronoun. It includes all the words in between.
> The engineer waved **from the speeding train**.

1. You can see the best railroad museum (in) the nation (in) Sacramento, California.

2. Locomotives and railroad cars show 150 years of railroad history.

3. Visitors can climb inside the displays and walk through them.

4. They can sit in the engineer's cab of a Santa Fe steam locomotive.

5. Visitors can experience the swaying motion of a Pullman sleeping car.

6. On some weekends, people can ride a steam train along the Sacramento River.

At the California State Railroad Museum in Sacramento, locomotives and railcars make railroad history come alive.

DIRECTIONS Add details to the paragraph. Choose prepositional phrases from the box. Then circle all the prepositions in the paragraph.

of a train whistle
in the sky
from our town
against our skin
in the darkness
of food and clothes

We rose (before) dawn and hurried (to) the railroad station

_____ (in) the darkness _____ . Stars shone faintly
             7.

_____ and the night air around us
            8.

felt cool _____ . The station was
            9.

crowded with other families _____ .
            10.

Mothers held crying babies in their arms. Fathers carried bags

_____ . Suddenly the sound
         11.

_____ split the air. The train roared into
         12.

the station. Soon, we were traveling to our new lives in the North.

GRAMMAR: COMPLEX SENTENCES

A Momentous Journey

Oil on canvas. Copyright © 1993 by The Museum of Modern Art, New York, and the Phillips Collection.

> ## Complex Sentences
>
> A **complex sentence** has one independent clause and one or more dependent clauses.
>
> An independent clause can stand alone as a sentence. The dependent clause often begins with a **subordinating conjunction**.
>
> **Because** many employees went to war,
>   dependent clause
> factories in the North needed new workers.
>   independent clause

DIRECTIONS Read each sentence. Underline the independent clause. Circle the dependent clause. Then write the subordinating conjunction.

1. (While life had always been hard for African Americans,) life got harder with the first World War.   _____While_____

2. The price of food doubled after the war began.   _____

3. Although slavery had been abolished, African Americans were still treated unfairly.   _____

4. Since Northern factories were recruiting Southerners, many African Americans headed north.   _____

5. When they left the South, African Americans expected big changes.   _____

6. It took courage to move to a place where nearly everything was new.   _____

7. Although it had its problems, the South was home to the African Americans.   _____

8. However, there were plenty of jobs in the North because workers had gone off to war.   _____

9. Northerners worked in factories while Southerners worked on farms.   _____

10. If they wanted jobs, the Southerners would have to learn new skills.   _____

11. Many people struggled a long time before things got better.   _____

12. Though it was not easy, they worked hard to improve their lives.   _____

SUM IT UP

Comparing and Summarizing

DIRECTIONS Review the comparison chart that you made about
"The Great Migration." Write *the same* or *different* to complete each
sentence. Then use details from your chart to explain the comparison.

1. Employment opportunities were _____different_____ in the North and the South.

   There were more jobs in the North than in the South.

2. Educational opportunities for African Americans were _____ in the North and the

   South. _____

3. Segregation was _____ in the North and the South.

   _____

4. The freedom to vote was _____ in the North and the South.

   _____

5. The cost of food was _____ in the North and the South.

   _____

DIRECTIONS Write a paragraph that compares life for African Americans
in the South and in the North. Include details from your chart.

Was life in the North mostly the same as in the South or mostly different?

Tell how things were alike and different in the South and the North. Use comparison words: *both, similar, same, but, however, not.*

Write a closing sentence.

Life for African Americans in the North was _____

life in the South. _____

_____

_____

_____

_____

_____

GRAMMAR: PHRASES AND CLAUSES

To the North by Train

DIRECTIONS Work with a partner. Take turns writing phrases, clauses, and sentences using the noun.

Phrases and Clauses

A **phrase** is a group of related words without a subject and a verb. A **clause** is a group of words with a subject and a verb.

> **phrase:** in the South
> **independent clause:** My family left the South.
> **dependent clause:** because life was hard

Clauses can be combined to form **compound sentences** and **complex sentences**.

> **compound:** My family lived in the South, **but** we moved to Pittsburgh.
> **complex:** We left the South **because** life was hard.

Example:

noun: train

prepositional phrase: by train

independent clause: Our families traveled by train.

compound sentence: Our families traveled by train, and we all arrived safely in the North.

complex sentence: Our families traveled by train until we arrived in the North.

1. **noun: city**

   prepositional phrase: _____

   independent clause: _____

   compound sentence: _____

   _____

   complex sentence: _____

Coordinating Conjunctions
and
but
or
for
yet

2. **noun: winter**

   prepositional phrase: _____

   independent clause: _____

   compound sentence: _____

   _____

   complex sentence: _____

   _____

A Few Subordinating Conjunctions
if
when
because
although
since
while
before

MORE ABOUT PHRASES AND CLAUSES Choose your own nouns. With your partner, take turns writing phrases, clauses, compound sentences, and complex sentences, as you did above.

Describe an Event

DIRECTIONS Choose one of Jacob Lawrence's paintings in your book. Imagine that you are part of the event. Write a description to tell what the event is like.

1 First list descriptive details about the event. Use the cluster. See Handbook page 409 for more about gathering details.

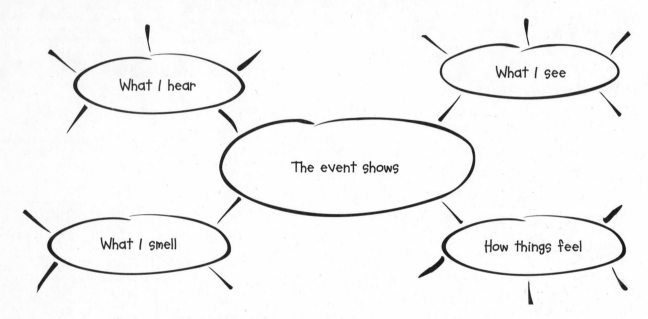

What I hear

What I see

The event shows

What I smell

How things feel

2 Organize your details. Show the order by adding numbers to the details in your cluster.

3 Write a description of the event.

Tell what the event is all about. _____

_____

Write the descriptive details in order. Make your reader believe that you are really there.

_____

_____

_____

Explain how you feel about what is happening.

_____

_____

_____

Research City Jobs

DIRECTIONS Complete the planner to help you and your group research jobs. Use the information to make a career notebook.

The Research Plan

Our group: _____

Our job category is: _____

The job we will research is: _____

_____ will look in the yellow pages
(Student's name) of a telephone book.

_____ will look for newspaper ads.
(Student's name)

_____ will look in library
(Student's name) reference books.

_____ will look on Web sites such as:
(Student's name) www.monster.com
www.flipdog.com/home.html

Yellow Pages Listing

Publishers-Book

Arrow Publishing
  P O Box 8574 Crml 555-1408
Benson Press 555-2120
Burton-Kelley Publishing Co
  611 Haven Rd PG 555-0638

Newspaper Ad

The Martin-Davis Company
A leading Educational Publishing Company,
is seeking an
Editor The right candidate will have at least four
years of experience in English language arts
publishing. Duties include writing, proofreading,

Reference Book

Occupation Outlook Handbook

My Research

Companies that hire for this job: _____

Skills and education required: _____

_____

Summary for our Career Notebook: _____

_____

_____

_____

_____

Taking Notes

DIRECTIONS Take notes about population growth in San Francisco during the Gold Rush. Follow the steps.

1 What do you want to know about the topic? Write a research question on each notecard on page 89.

2 Read the magazine article to learn about the topic.

> **Taking Notes**
>
> **Taking notes** will help you remember and organize information that you find. Your notes will also help you remember the sources of your information.

The Sudden Growth of San Francisco

By JAMES FOLEY

In the mid 1840s, San Francisco was a sleepy little frontier town called Yerba Buena. Then, in 1848, gold was discovered on the American River. At first, there was no race to California—people did not believe the tales of gold. Then government officials reported that the rumors were true. Newspapers spread the word. Horace Greeley of the *New York Tribune* reported: "Fortune lies upon the surface of the earth as plentiful as the mud in our streets."

The rush began. Thousands of gold-seekers traveled to California. Many professional men, merchants, and entertainers came to sell goods or services to the miners.

People came from everywhere. Americans from the eastern United States traveled by ship or took the overland route in wagons and on foot. Either trip could take several months. Gold-seekers sailed to California from throughout the world. Most of the ships arrived at the port of San Francisco.

Sacramento Street, San Francisco, circa 1855.

San Francisco changed quickly. It became an important supply center. It became a city of many cultures. It had theater, opera, and more newspapers than any other city in America. The population of San Francisco was 800 in January, 1848. By 1860, it was 56,802.

—from *California History*, Feb. 16, 2001 (Vol.4, No.1)

---

3 Take notes. Include at least one quotation from the article.
For more about note-taking, see Handbook page 396.

Notecards

Research Question

Source

Notes

4 Use your notes to tell a partner about San Francisco's growth during the gold rush.

Reaching Freedom

New Words

- capture
- conductor
- escape
- freedom
- journey
- network
- reward
- runaway slave
- slavery

Use New Words in Context

DIRECTIONS Use the new words to finish the paragraph.

In the early history of the United States, _____ was

1.

legal. Some African American slaves tried to _____ .

2.

A _____ often used the Underground Railroad. It was

3.

a _____ of people and places that helped these slaves.

4.

The _____ on the Underground Railroad was dangerous.

5.

Slave hunters tried to _____ some slaves. So the slaves

6.

needed a _____ to guide them north. There, they hoped

7.

to find _____ . This was the _____

8.   9.

that waited for them at the end of their long journey.

Relate Words

DIRECTIONS Write sentences about each topic. Use two new words
in each sentence.

Topics	Sentences
10. Losing freedom	
11. Getting away	
12. Working together	
13. A railroad trip	
14. Something good	

© Hampton-Brown

Train to Freedom

Harriet Tubman was born around 1820 and died in 1913. She made several rescue trips on the Underground Railroad and helped guide many slaves to freedom.

Indefinite Adjectives

Use an **indefinite adjective** when you don't know the exact amount of something.

To Tell How Many:
many	no	several
some	a few	

That night, **several** slaves traveled the Underground Railroad together.

To Tell How Much:
much	no	some
a little	not much	

With **a little** imagination, they could feel The tracks beneath their feet.

DIRECTIONS Circle the indefinite adjective in each sentence. Decide if the adjective tells *how many* or *how much*. Check the correct column.

	How Many?	**How Much?**
1. (Several) people joined the Underground Railroad to help slaves.	✔	
2. The Underground Railroad gave slaves a little hope.	_____	_____
3. Conductors, such as Harriet Tubman and Peg Leg Joe, guided many slaves north.	_____	_____
4. It took much courage to secretly help slaves.	_____	_____
5. The conductors probably felt some fear for their own lives.	_____	_____
6. Peg Leg Joe taught several slaves the song "Follow the Drinking Gourd."	_____	_____
7. The lyrics of the song contained many clues to help slaves on their journey.	_____	_____
8. A few clues told which season was best for traveling.	_____	_____
9. Some information was about the trail to follow.	_____	_____
10. Slaves traveled by night, when there was not much light.	_____	_____
11. It was especially dark on nights with no moonlight.	_____	_____
12. Some slaves were captured and sent back.	_____	_____

Apparent Message and Hidden Agenda

DIRECTIONS With a partner, look back at the song on page 186.
Then complete the chart.

Apparent Message	Hidden Agenda
The riverbank makes a very good road,	Walk along the riverbank.
The dead trees will show you the way.	Follow the dead trees.

DIRECTIONS Talk about the hidden agendas with your partner. Then draw a
map for the slaves to follow.

© Hampton-Brown

Home Words

New Words

flat

landlord

laundromat

ordinary

own

real

rent

temporary

washroom

Relate Words

DIRECTIONS Write new words to complete each chart.

Antonyms	
false	
permanent	
	borrow
special	

Synonyms	
apartment	
bathroom	
laundry	
	payment

Use New Words in Context

DIRECTIONS Use the new words to complete the paragraph.

I used to think my life was _____ordinary_____.
                                    1.

My family _____ a house in the
                    2.

country. Now we pay _____ for a
                          3.

small _____ in the city. Life is very
         4.

different here. Instead of hanging clothes in the fresh

Our house in the country.

air, we use a _____. We don't even have our own
                  5.

bathroom; we have to use the _____ down the hall.
                                  6.

Our _____ is very kind, but we hardly know our
       7.

neighbors. It's like a sad dream. Nothing seems _____
                                                    8.

here. It all feels _____, like it could change any minute.
                      9.

My country home doesn't seem so _____ now.
                                        10.

Stories and Dreams

DIRECTIONS Read each pair of sentences. Complete the second sentence with a helping verb from the box. Use a different helping verb in each sentence.

Some Helping Verbs					
could	would	should	may	might	will

Helping Verbs

A **helping verb** is a small word that comes before a **main verb**. Some helping verbs tell about things that are possible, not things that are definite.

She **would** like a home of her own.
She **will** make her dream come true.

1. Sandra Cisneros writes about the lives of Mexican Americans.

   She ____would____ like people to know about their lives.

2. She will probably continue writing in the future. She _____ write several more novels.

3. You ought to write a story, too. You _____ tell about your own experiences.

4. It is possible that your story will be good. It _____ be great!

5. My mother plans to write our family history. She _____ write about our ancestors.

6. Many of our relatives live nearby. She _____ interview them!

DIRECTIONS Write a paragraph about your dream house. Tell about the possibilities. Use a helping verb in each sentence.

I would like _____

_____

_____

_____

_____

_____

_____

_____

Esperanza's Dream

> **Two-Word Verbs**
>
> A **two-word verb** is a verb followed by a small word. The meaning of a two-word verb is different from the meaning of the verb by itself.
>
> **Turn** right at the corner.
> **Turn off** the radio.

DIRECTIONS Work with a partner. Complete each sentence. Write the correct word. Use the list of two-word verbs and their meanings on Handbook pages 452–453 to help you.

1. Esperanza wants to **get** _____ahead_____ in life.
   <u>over / ahead</u>

2. She **looks** _____ to a better future.
   <u>forward / over</u>

3. She wants to live in a house where things don't **break** _____.
   <u>down / out</u>

4. When the pipes broke, her family **ran** _____ of water.
   <u>into / out</u>

5. What else will **give** _____ in the house?
   <u>in / out</u>

6. To Esperanza, her house **stands** _____ failure.
   <u>for / out</u>

7. She wants to **get** _____ of her crumbling
   <u>out / along</u>
   neighborhood.

8. When she imagines the future, she **fills** _____ the
   <u>in / out</u>
   pictures in her head with bright colors.

9. She sees a pretty house that **stands** _____ on
   <u>for / out</u>
   a nice street.

10. Esperanza will not **give** _____ on her dream.
    <u>up / out</u>

In "A House of My Own," Esperanza tells of her dreams for the future.

MORE ABOUT TWO-WORD VERBS Make up sentences with two-word verbs. Read them to your partner. Then listen to your partner's sentences.

GRAMMAR: COMPLEX SENTENCES

Meet Mary Helen Ponce

DIRECTIONS Read the article. Underline each complex sentence.

<u>Mary Helen Ponce loves Pacoima, California, where she was born in 1938.</u> She grew up in a big Mexican American family, and she had a happy childhood. She has fond memories of her childhood.

Mary Helen loved to read and considered books her best friends. Since she read constantly, she learned how to write. When she was young, she wrote all the time—"either on paper or in the dirt," she says.

When Mary Helen grew up, she got married and had four children. She read books and wrote stories while she raised her family. In 1974, she decided to go to college. After she became a teacher, she published her first book. It was a collection of stories about Mexican Americans.

Today, Mary Helen is very busy. She writes, reads books, gives readings, and conducts lectures. If she has time, she communicates on-line with writers and readers.

> ### Complex Sentences
>
> A **complex sentence** has one independent clause and one or more dependent clauses.
>
> An independent clause can stand alone as a sentence. The dependent clause in a complex sentence often begins with a **subordinating conjunction**.
>
> <u>Mary Helen has warm memories of the town</u>
>   independent clause
> **where** she grew up.
>   dependent clause

When Mary Helen Ponce was young, she decided that she wanted to be a writer.

DIRECTIONS Write a complex sentence to answer each question about the article. Underline the subordinating conjunction.

1. How did Mary Helen feel during her childhood? _Mary Helen felt happy <u>when</u> she was growing up._

_____

2. Why do you think Mary Helen considered books to be her best friends? _____

_____

3. How did Mary Helen learn to write? _____

_____

4. When did Mary Helen publish her first book? _____

_____

5. Does Mary Helen use the Internet? _____

© Hampton-Brown

Say It With Style!

Style and Word Choice

Word choice is one element of an author's **style**. Authors choose words carefully to express ideas and feelings clearly.

DIRECTIONS Work with a partner. Read the passages. Which passage expresses ideas and feelings more clearly? Underline the effective word choices. Then complete the sentence.

The Living Room

This room must look shabby to a stranger. The couch is old. The rugs and coverings are old. The pillows are flat and dirty. An ice cream sundae is just about to spill.

I know this room well. This is a happy room. I remember story times and games. I see a room I like.

Nanny's Living Room

A stranger's eyes see a shabby room. They see a shipwreck of a couch, washed up onto the sandy beach of Nanny's living room. Their eyes take in tired threads, stuffing, fluff, flat-tire pillows, drained and stained. They watch a waterfall of ice creamy fudge. Splash! Smudge!

My familiar eyes see a chuckling, hugging, living space. This is a lively room, filled with words and the twists and turns of love and life. I see a loving room, filled with caring and sharing.

The word choices in " _____ " are more effective because

_____

_____

DIRECTIONS Write sentences that describe a bedroom. What effective word choices could replace the ordinary words? Read page 416 in the Handbook for ideas. Share your description with a partner.

Ordinary Words			
small bed	long curtains	big window	messy desk
regular chair	full closet	plain mirror	open door

_____

_____

_____

Make Inferences

DIRECTIONS Work with a partner. Follow the steps to make
inferences and predict an outcome.

1 **Confirm Word Meanings** Use word parts, context, or a dictionary to confirm
the meaning of each underlined word. Then tell how you confirmed the meaning.

2 **Make Inferences** When you make an inference, you add what you know to better
understand what the author means. Write what the author means but does not say.

Story Passage	How I Confirmed Meaning	Inference
The house on Mango Street is ours, and we don't have to pay <u>rent</u> to anybody.	dictionary	They didn't like paying rent to someone else. They are happy to own their home.
Out back is a small <u>garage</u> for the car we don't own yet.		
And so she <u>trudged</u> up the wooden stairs, her sad brown shoes taking her to the house she never liked.		
But she doesn't know which subway train to take to get <u>downtown</u>.		
This was the house Papa talked about when he held a <u>lottery ticket</u>.		

3 **Predict an Outcome** Write a paragraph that predicts whether Esperanza will
come back to Mango Street. Explain your thinking. Share your paragraph
with another pair of students.

_____

_____

_____

_____

As Pretty as a Picture

DIRECTIONS Look at each picture. Use the clues to complete each simile.

> **Similes**
>
> A **simile** uses the words *like* or *as* to compare one thing to another.
>   The apartment smelled **as fresh as spring rain.**
>   She moved **like a broken-down shopping cart.**

The new quilt looks as cheerful as ____a circus tent____ .
                                      (something bright and fun)

The quilt feels as warm as _____ .
                            (something in nature)

The old quilt smells like _____ .
                           (a food)

The leaves shine like _____ .
                       (jewels)

The tree looks as tall as _____ .
                           (a building)

The wind through the branches sounds like _____ .
                                           (something noisy)

DIRECTIONS Write similes to describe the scene.

1. How small was the cabin? The cabin looked as tiny as

   _____ .

2. How did the chimney look? _____

   _____

3. How did the stairs sound? _____

   _____

4. How did the cabin smell? _____

   _____

RESEARCH SKILLS

Using Charts

> **Charts**
>
> **Charts** can help you organize a lot of information in a small space. Charts have rows, columns, and labels to display information.

DIRECTIONS Create a chart to display information.

1 **Read about John's survey.**

Several students in John's class have lived in or traveled to New York City. John wanted to know which famous places they had visited there. He took a survey. This is what he found out:

- Ken has been to the Statue of Liberty and to the Empire State Building.
- Lena has walked through Central Park. She has also seen an exhibit at the Museum of Modern Art.
- Joyce has been to Times Square and to the top of the Empire State Building. She has gone on a field trip to the Museum of Modern Art, too.
- Leo has seen a baseball game at Yankee Stadium.
- Kise has been to all the places the other students have visited.

2 **Make a chart to show the information from the survey. What labels will you write at the top of each column? How many columns and rows will you need?**

Title: _____

3 **What are the benefits of using a chart? Explain what it helps you to do.**

_____

_____

_____

_____

_____

© Hampton-Brown

CONTENT AREA CONNECTIONS

Evaluate Web Sites

New York City

DIRECTIONS Work with a partner. Follow the steps to evaluate Web sites.

1 Choose two cities where you would like to live. Explore Web sites that give information about them.

City 1: _____ City 2: _____

2 Choose one Web site for each city. Write the addresses at the top of the chart. Evaluate both sites. Complete the chart.

What to Look For	Web site 1: _____	Web site 2: _____
Is the site attractive? Describe how photos, graphics, sound, and animation are used.		
Can you find the information quickly? Is the text easy to read? Explain.		
Is the information interesting, useful, and complete? Explain.		
How helpful are the links to other sites? Is there an e-mail link?		

3 Share your opinions about the Web sites with the class.

Continuity and Change

DIRECTIONS Answer the questions about "Continuity" and "Change" on the mind map. Add more ideas to the map as you read the selections in this unit.

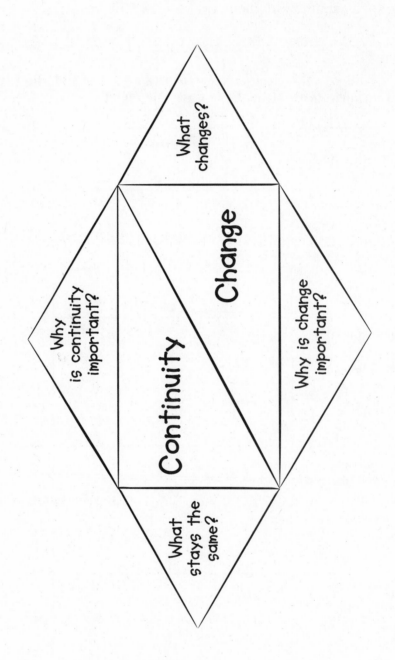

Tell Us About the Parthenon

The Parthenon sits on the Acropolis, which is a hill overlooking Athens.

> ### Relative Clauses
>
> A **relative clause** is one kind of dependent clause. It is used with an independent clause to make a complex sentence.
>
> Ictinus and Callicrates were the architects **who designed the Parthenon.**
>
> A **relative pronoun** begins a relative clause. Use **who, whom,** or **whose** for people. Use **which** for things. Use **that** for people or things.
>
> The Parthenon, **which** sits on the Acropolis, overlooks Athens.

DIRECTIONS Underline the relative clauses. Circle the relative pronouns.

1. The Parthenon is a famous Greek temple (that) was built nearly 2,500 years ago.

2. It was built to honor Athena, who was the Greek goddess of wisdom.

3. The Greeks often built temples to gods whom they wanted to please.

4. Athena, whose statue used to sit inside the Parthenon, was the patron goddess of Athens.

5. The temple was built entirely of white marble, which was brought from a nearby mountain.

6. The Parthenon, which still dominates the Acropolis, now shows us only some of its former beauty.

7. The columns, which were carved in the Doric style, are still standing today.

8. However, the brightly colored sculptures that decorated the ends of the roof are gone.

9. The eastern end had scenes that showed the birth of Athena.

10. Other sculptures showed centaurs and amazons, which are part of Greek mythology.

11. A decorated strip, which is known as a frieze, showed Athenians in a procession.

12. People who travel to Athens today learn a lot about ancient Greek culture.

Words About Seasons

New Words

bear fruit

damp

dull

gloomy

shiver

shrivel up

sprout

underworld

wither

Relate Words

DIRECTIONS Draw a picture of summertime in the upper part of the circle. Draw wintertime in the lower part. Use the new words to write a sentence about each season.

Summer is when _____

_____ .

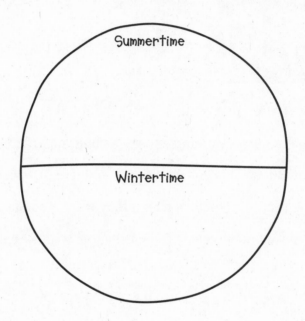

Winter is _____

_____ .

Use New Words in Context

DIRECTIONS Write a new word to complete each sentence.

1. The _____ is the home of the dead.

2. No one laughs in that sad and _____ place.

3. The chilly air is moist and _____ .

4. People shake and _____ with cold.

5. Nothing sparkles or shines on the _____ walls.

6. Seeds do not _____ in the barren fields.

Gods and Goddesses

DIRECTIONS Read the sentences about Greek gods and goddesses. Combine the sentences using *which* or *that*.

> ### Relative Clauses
> A **relative clause** is one kind of dependent clause. It is used with an independent clause to make a complex sentence. A relative clause begins with a relative pronoun like **that** or **which**.
>
> Demeter ruled over all **that grew**.
> Winged sandals, **which helped him fly**, were Hermes' trademark.

1. The bridle was invented by Athena. The bridle allows people to ride horses. (**which**)

   The bridle, which allows people to ride horses, was invented by Athena.

   _____

2. Zeus had a thunderbolt. Zeus hurled his thunderbolt at his enemies. (**that**)

   _____

   _____

3. The golden lyre was played by Apollo. The golden lyre is a stringed instrument. (**which**)

   _____

   _____

4. Artemis had silver arrows. She shot the arrows from her bow. (**which**)

   _____

   _____

5. Poseidon ruled the angry waves. The angry waves crashed on the shore. (**that**)

   _____

   _____

6. Hades ruled the underworld. The underworld was a dark and dismal kingdom. (**which**)

   _____

   _____

Name _____   Date _____

Favorite Seasons

DIRECTIONS Write relative pronouns to complete the sentences.

> **Relative Clauses**
>
> A **relative clause** is used with an independent clause to make a complex sentence. A relative clause begins with a **relative pronoun**. Use **who** for people. Use **that** for people or things.
>
> I went sledding with Lisa, **who has a cabin.**
> The friends **that she invites** all like snow.
> The season **that I like best** is winter.

1. Denise, _____who_____ loves summertime, likes to swim.

2. Her friends _____ are on swim teams practice every day.

3. Luis, _____ thinks summer is too hot, prefers the autumn.

4. He likes to rake the leaves _____ fall to the ground.

5. He plays football with Jarrod, _____ lives next door.

6. Fred, _____ likes winter best, is learning to ski.

7. A train _____ goes to the mountains takes him skiing every weekend.

8. His friends _____ know how to ski go with him.

DIRECTIONS Complete each sentence with a relative clause. Begin the clause with *who* or *that*.

9. Soraya, _____who lives with her grandmother_____ , loves to garden.

10. Her grandmother, _____ , teaches her many things.

11. Soraya gives plants to groups

    _____ .

12. People _____ look forward to spring.

MORE ABOUT RELATIVE CLAUSES Circle *who* or *that* in each sentence. Draw an arrow to the word it tells about.

Mrs. Okutani teaches Soraya how to grow *bonsai* trees for people who are sick.

© Hampton-Brown

Characters, Problems, and Solutions

DIRECTIONS Work with a partner. Complete the chart for each character. Brainstorm other possible solutions and consequences to add to the chart.

Demeter

Problem	
Solution	
Consequence	
Other Solution	
Other Consequence	

Persephone

Problem	
Solution	
Consequence	
Other Solution	
Other Consequence	

Parts of a Plot

DIRECTIONS Complete the plot diagram.

> **Plot**
> Most stories have several parts.
> - The **conflict** is the story problem.
> - During the **rising action**, events lead to a climax. **Complications** are events that make the problem more difficult; the **climax** is the turning point when you learn about the outcome.
> - During the **falling action**, events lead to a resolution. The **resolution** answers the remaining questions about the story.

The Mother Who Lost Her Daughter

Characters: _____

Setting: _____

Climax: _____
_____

Complication:

Persephone eats _____

_____

Complication:

Demeter feels so sad that _____

_____

RISING ACTION

FALLING ACTION

Resolution: _____
_____
_____
_____

Conflict: _____

_____

WRITING: A MYTH

And That Explains Why . . .

> **Myth**
>
> A **myth** is a very old story that explains something about the world. Myths tell how gods and goddesses made natural events happen.

DIRECTIONS Write a myth that explains something in nature.

1 **Brainstorm Natural Events** Choose an event to explain, such as why the sun rises and sets, or why earthquakes happen.

2 **Choose a Greek God or Goddess** Select one from page 219 of your book, or invent one. Make a character map.

3 **Write a Myth** You might use a story map to organize your ideas. See Handbook pages 375–377. Now write your myth.

Title: _____

Tell about the setting, characters, and **conflict**.

_____

_____

_____

_____

Describe the **rising action** that leads to the story's turning point. Include **complications**.

_____

_____

_____

_____

Write the **climax** and describe the **falling action**. Be sure to end the story with a **resolution**.

_____

_____

_____

_____

© Hampton-Brown

CONTENT AREA CONNECTIONS

Study Behavior and Nature

DIRECTIONS Work with a group. Follow the steps to study how nature affects human behavior.

1 **Think About Natural Events** Add one natural event to the chart. Write how each event affects people's behavior.

Natural Event	Effect
very hot weather	
thunder and lightning	
hurricane	
beautiful spring day	
snow	
longer days	
_____	

2 **Write a Hypothesis** A hypothesis is a statement that you will try to prove. Choose one event from the chart above. Write a hypothesis that explains what your group wants to prove.

We want to prove that _____

_____

_____ .

3 **Conduct Research** Gather information from different sources to find out more about the event.

- Use library sources such as encyclopedias, almanacs, and scientific journals.

- Interview people.

People spend more time outdoors in warm weather.

© Hampton-Brown

• Make observations and pay attention to how people behave. Take notes.

Observation Form

Date and time: _____

Place: _____

The people I observed: _____

What I observed or found out: _____

People organize festivals to brighten the dark days of winter.

4 **Draw a Conclusion** Did your research and observations prove the hypothesis? If not, write a new hypothesis to match what you learned. Explain how your data proves the hypothesis.

_____

_____

_____

_____

_____

5 **Explain Your Results** As a group, review all of the data you collected. Decide what your final hypothesis will be. Then present the results of your study to the class.

Final hypothesis: _____

_____

Butterfly Words

Use Context Clues

New Words

caterpillar
cease
chronicle
chrysalis
dangle
diary
dissolve
fasten
reshape
shed
vanish

DIRECTIONS Rewrite the paragraph. Replace each underlined definition with the correct form of a new word.

The <u>Life Story</u> of a Butterfly

A butterfly starts as a tiny egg, then changes into a <u>worm-like creature</u>. The caterpillar <u>hooks</u> onto a plant. Then it <u>loses</u> its skin and becomes an <u>insect enclosed in a hard shell</u>. The chrysalis <u>hangs down loosely</u> from the plant. Inside, the chrysalis <u>completely changes</u> itself. Its old body parts <u>disappear</u> and it grows wings. It <u>stops</u> being a caterpillar or a chrysalis. It is now a butterfly. It comes out, flies away, and <u>fades from view</u>.

_____

_____

_____

_____

_____

_____

_____

_____

_____

_____

_____

Constant Consonants

DIRECTIONS Read the poem with a partner. Write each example of alliteration and consonance in the chart. Underline the letters whose sounds are repeated.

Alliteration and Consonance

Alliteration is the repetition of consonant sounds at the beginnings of words.

the <u>c</u>ocoon <u>c</u>radles the <u>ch</u>rysalis

Consonance is the repetition of a consonant sound in the middle or at the end of words that have different vowel sounds.

the sa<u>p</u> cree<u>ps</u> u<u>p</u>ward

Poets use alliteration and consonance to emphasize feelings and ideas or to create a musical sound.

Bear and Butterfly
— E. C. Sengel

The bear in its winter bed
The chrysalis in its cocoon
Sleep through silent days,
Miss the magic of the moon.

The bear's heart fondly remembers
Summer slopes where berries lie;
The chrysalis carries a tender dream
Of lifting wings upon the sky.

When snows melt in the mountains
And fish flash in the stream,
The forest calls the sleepy bear.
Winter passes like a dream.

Butterfly sheds its weary shell
And fans each weightless wing,
As delicate as blossoms,
They open to the spring.

Alliteration	Consonance In the middle of words	Consonance At the end of words
<u>B</u>ear, <u>B</u>utterfly, <u>b</u>ed	chrysa<u>l</u>is, si<u>l</u>ent	bea<u>r</u>, winte<u>r</u>

Steps in a Process

DIRECTIONS Read the passage. Then write the steps of the cycle in the diagram.

The Life Cycle of the Pacific Salmon

In summer or fall, thousands of adult salmon leave their ocean home and struggle upstream to the places where they were born. The females lay their eggs in the rocky bottom of a stream. The males fertilize the eggs. Then both the parents die.

In the spring, the salmon eggs hatch. After they grow bigger, the young salmon migrate downstream to the ocean.

Birds, commercial fishers, pollution, dams, and other dangers make the long journey difficult for the salmon. Very few reach the sea.

The young salmon that survive grow into adults in the ocean. After several years, both males and females return upstream to their birthplaces. Then the cycle begins again.

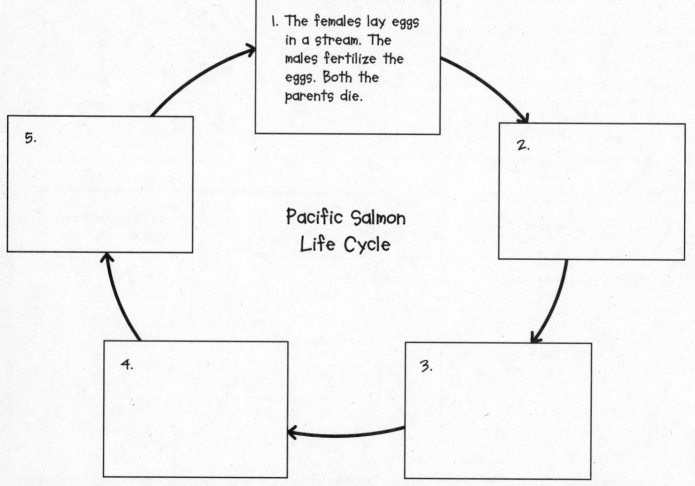

1. The females lay eggs in a stream. The males fertilize the eggs. Both the parents die.

5.

2.

Pacific Salmon
Life Cycle

4.

3.

Volcanic Words

New Words

avalanche
colonizer
crater
dome
earthquake
eruption
flow
force
lava
magma
pressure
survivor

Use New Words in Context

DIRECTIONS Make a four-square diagram for each new word.

Word: avalanche	Picture:
Definition:	Sentence:

Word: magma	Picture:
Definition:	Sentence:

Word: crater	Picture:
Definition:	Sentence:

Word: flow	Picture:
Definition:	Sentence:

Word: lava	Picture:
Definition:	Sentence:

Word: force	Picture:
Definition:	Sentence:

Images in the Mind

DIRECTIONS Underline the two objects being compared in each simile. Describe the image it creates in your mind.

> **Similes**
>
> A **simile** uses *like* or *as* to compare two things. It creates a clear mental image in the mind of the reader.
>
> Mount St. Helens was **like a giant pressure cooker.**

Simile	**Mental Image**
1. The <u>mountain</u> swelled like a <u>balloon</u>.	The mountain got bigger and bigger until it burst.
2. The forest was as smoky as a thousand chimneys.	
3. A boulder as heavy as a train engine tumbled across the road.	
4. The wind screamed like some gigantic parrot.	
5. The avalanche raced down the mountain like a champion skier.	
6. Ash as pale as snow fell across the countryside.	

DIRECTIONS Work with a partner. Read each sentence. Use the underlined words to help you form a mental image. Brainstorm other objects that are like your image. Then write a simile to complete the sentence.

7. <u>Without her trees and plants</u> Mount St. Helens looks _as bare as an egg_____ .

8. Then the mountain begins to <u>awaken slowly</u> from her slumber _____

_____ .

9. Ants, mice, and squirrels <u>scatter seeds</u> across the landscape _____

_____ .

10. Within a few years, Mount St. Helens bursts into <u>patterns of color</u> _____

_____ .

© Hampton-Brown

It Happened Suddenly

DIRECTIONS Read the adverbs in the box. Write each adverb under the correct heading.

high	underground	violently	quickly
again	often	downward	later
safely	dangerously	sideways	early

> **Adverbs**
>
> An **adverb** tells *how*, *where*, or *when*. An adverb usually describes a verb.
>
> Mudflows traveled **swiftly**. (how)
> Ash blew **eastward**. (where)
> Life returned **soon**. (when)

How

1. ____violently____

2. _____

3. _____

4. _____

When

5. _____

6. _____

7. _____

8. _____

Where

9. _____

10. _____

11. _____

12. _____

DIRECTIONS Work with a partner. Add details to the sentences. Include adverbs from the box above or adverbs of your own.

13. Mount St. Helens erupted ___violently on May 18, 1980___

_____.

14. A blast of steam shot _____

_____.

15. The second eruption blew ash and rock _____

_____.

16. Hot pumice and ash flowed _____

_____.

17. Some animals stayed _____

_____.

18. In 1980, the mountain erupted _____

Mount St. Helens erupted violently on May 18, 1980. This view is from Gifford-Pinchot National Forest in Washington State.

Eyewitness to Disaster

DIRECTIONS Read the article. Underline each sentence that has a relative clause.

> **Relative Clauses**
>
> A **relative clause** is used with an independent clause to make a complex sentence. It begins with a **relative pronoun**. Use **who** for people. Use **that** for people or things.
>
> May is a journalist **who wrote about the blast**.
> Journalists **that visited the site** risked their lives.
> The blast **that flattened forests** carried boulders.

Reporter Tells of Disaster

On the morning of May 18, 1980, journalist Bud May received a call from a relative who lived in Toutle, Washington. The news that May heard was startling. Mount St. Helens had erupted.

The caller, who could see Mount St. Helens from her house, described the mountain. A huge black cloud, slashed by lightning, hung near the summit.

May and his wife, who lived nearby in Castle Rock, hurried down to the Cowlitz River. They gathered with other people who lived in the area. A scanner crackled with reports of a mudflow that was rushing down the Toutle River valley. The river of mud was sweeping up houses, vehicles, animals, and trees. Sheriff's deputies were trying to evacuate residents that lived in the path of danger. Fish were trying to jump out of the heated waters of the Cowlitz.

May will never forget that terrible day. Today he works in the Castle Rock Exhibit Hall. He enjoys talking to tourists who are on their way to see the famous volcano.

DIRECTIONS Study the relative clause in each underlined sentence in the article above. Write the relative pronoun. Then write the noun that the clause describes.

1. ____who____   ____relative____

2. _____   _____

3. _____   _____

4. _____   _____

5. _____   _____

6. _____   _____

7. _____   _____

8. _____   _____

Bud May worked on a newspaper that covered the eruption of Mount St. Helens.

© Hampton-Brown

Relate Causes and Effects

DIRECTIONS Compare "The Big Blast" to "The Mother Who Lost Her Daughter."

1 Review your notecards about "The Big Blast." Finish the chart.

Causes	→	Effects
An earthquake happens.	→	An avalanche tears open the mountain.
Steam blasts from the volcano.	→	
	→	There are huge mudflows.
Lava flows out of the vent.	→	
	→	The dome gets bigger.

2 Answer the questions about the two changes in each selection.

"The Big Blast"	"The Mother Who Lost Her Daughter"
How did Mount St. Helens change after the eruptions? _____ _____	How did Earth change after Hades took Persephone to the underworld? _____ _____
What is Mount St. Helens like today? _____ _____	How did Earth change again after Persephone returned? _____ _____

3 Write a sentence that tells how the changes in the two selections are the same.

_____

_____

4 Tell how the selections are different.

_____

_____

LANGUAGE ARTS CONNECTIONS

Exploring Our Roots

DIRECTIONS Work in a group of five. Use the meanings of Latin and Greek roots to expand your English vocabulary.

1 Complete the chart. Write as many words as you can that contain the root.

Latin and Greek Roots

Recognizing **Latin and Greek roots** can help you understand the meanings of new words.

Root	Meaning	English Words
bio	life	biology
pop	people	population

Latin and Greek Roots

Root	Meaning	Examples
geo	earth	geologist, geothermal, geography, geometry, geology, geodesic dome, geophysics, geological, geode, geocentric
photo	light	
graph	written	
rupt	break	
dict	say	
viv	live	
sci	know	

© Hampton-Brown

2 **Read the passage. Look at the underlined words.**

A Volcano Erupts! Geography Changes.

When the Nevado del Ruiz volcano erupted in 1985, thousands of Colombians lost their lives. The geography of the region was changed.

Nine kilometers from the summit, scientists used a seismograph to monitor the volcano. They wanted to help people survive a future blast. In October, the Colombian Institute of Geology and Mines issued a warning about a possible eruption. However, the government chose not to make people leave. Officials were not convinced of immediate danger, and they did not want to disrupt residents' lives.

When the volcano exploded on November 13th, tons of debris swept down the mountain. The flow was bad, as

On November 13, 1985, Nevado del Ruiz erupted in South America. Eighty-five percent of the town of Armero, Columbia, was covered with debris.

agencies had predicted. Many people had believed they would be safe. The facts contradicted that belief. The blast did more than interrupt lives. In Armero, 23,000 people died. The photograph above shows the town of Armero after the blast.

3 **Have each group member write definitions for two of the underlined words. Use the roots to guess their meanings; then check the definitions in a dictionary.**

_____

_____

_____

_____

_____

_____

_____

_____

4 **Share your definitions with the group. Use each word in a sentence.**

_____

Before and After

> ### News Story
>
> A **news story** is an article that gives facts about a current event. A **headline** is a line of large print at the top of a news article. It tells in a few words what the article is about.

DIRECTIONS Write a news story about an imaginary event at Mount St. Helens the day before the eruption. Then write one about an event on the day after the eruption.

1 **Choose Topics** You might write about an activity such as fishing or camping, or about a job such as forest ranger or scientist. Choose related topics for your stories.

2 **Write Your First Story** Write about an event before the eruption.

Write a short **headline** that gives the main idea of your story. It should tell what the story is about.

_____

_____

_____

In the **lead paragraph**, give the most important information about the event. Answer the questions *Who? What? Where? When? Why?* and *How?*

_____

_____

_____

_____

_____

Report more facts and interesting details. Make sure you do not include your personal feelings about what happened.

_____

_____

_____

_____

_____

_____

_____

3 **Write Your Second Story** Write about a related event that happened the day after the eruption.

4 **Edit and Publish Your Work** You might type your articles on a computer in the style of a news article.

Using Maps

DIRECTIONS Work with a partner. Look at the map of the state of Washington. Then read the list below. Label each place on the map.

Western Washington

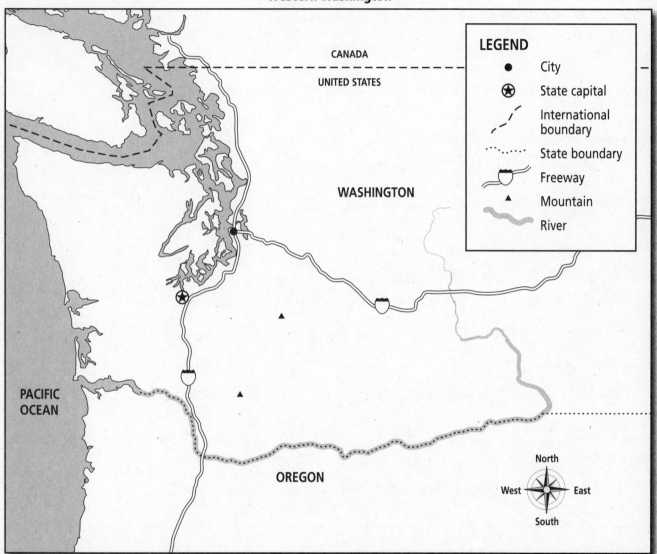

1. Olympia, the state capital

2. Seattle, the largest city

3. Puget Sound, the body of water west of Seattle

4. Mt. Rainier, east of Olympia

5. Mt. St. Helens in southern Washington

6. The Columbia River, marking the boundary between Oregon and Washington

7. Interstate 5, the main north-south freeway in the western part of the state

8. Interstate 90, the main freeway leading east from Seattle

CONTENT AREA CONNECTIONS

Make a Volcano Report

Eruption of Mount St. Helens, May 18, 1980

DIRECTIONS With a group, research a volcanic eruption. Then make a map to help you report your findings to the class.

1 **Choose a Volcano** You might research Etna, Kilauea, Krakatoa, Mauna Loa, Mount Shasta, or Vesuvius.

Volcano: _____

2 **Find Information** Use a variety of sources. Answer the questions with your group.

• What was the date of the eruption? _____

• Describe the eruption. How long did it last? How did the volcano's shape change? _____

_____

_____

_____

• How did the eruption affect the natural environment? _____

_____

_____

• How did the eruption affect nearby cities and the people living there? _____

_____

_____

• Have there been other major eruptions of the volcano? Give the dates. _____

_____

• Is the volcano dormant now, or is it active? _____

3 **Organize the Information** Write key facts on notecards to use in your presentation.

4 **Create a Map** Make a map that is large enough for the class to see.

• Label the volcano, country, cities that were affected, and bodies of water.

• Include a compass rose and a legend.

5 **Give Your Report** Present your map and information to the class.

© Hampton-Brown

BUILD LANGUAGE AND VOCABULARY

Explain It to Me

DIRECTIONS Complete each sentence. Write the present perfect tense of the verb in parentheses. See Handbook pages 450–451 for a list of irregular past participles.

1. Airplanes _____have changed_____ greatly since World War II. (**change**)

2. Planes like the British Spitfire and the German Messerschmitt _____ obsolete. (**become**)

3. Something _____ obsolete when it is out-of-date or no longer useful. (**become**)

4. These old aircraft have become obsolete because aircraft technology _____ sleeker, faster planes. (**develop**)

5. Improvements in wing design _____ the speed and range of some planes. (**increase**)

6. Engineers _____ "stealth" airplanes that can avoid radar detection. (**build**)

7. Many people _____ about the history of airplanes through museums. (**learn**)

8. The National Air and Space Museum _____ many visitors. (**attract**)

9. The museum _____ an exhibition gallery to the fliers and planes of World War II. (**dedicate**)

10. These historic planes may be obsolete, but they _____ many visitors. (**thrill**)

> ## Present Perfect Tense
>
> The **present perfect tense** can tell about an action that happened at an unknown time in the past. To form the present perfect tense, use **has** or **have** and the **past participle**.
>
> Planes **have changed** since World War II.
>
> Regular past participles end in **–ed**. Irregular past participles vary in their form.
>
> Milo **has** <u>visited</u> the space museum. He **has** <u>seen</u> many historic planes.

The British Spitfire is a legendary World War II fighter plane. Planes like these have become obsolete.

World War II Words

New Words

annex

concentration camp

declare war on

discriminate against

law

power

prisoner

survive

Use Definitions

DIRECTIONS Write the new words next to their definitions.

1. rule that controls what you are allowed to do _____

2. stay alive at a difficult time _____

3. part of a building that is added on _____

4. person who is locked up and guarded _____

5. announce plan to fight against a country _____

6. place for keeping prisoners of war _____

7. treat someone unfairly _____

Use New Words in Context

DIRECTIONS Use the new words to finish the paragraph.

After Adolf Hitler gained _____ in Germany in 1933, he took
                                    8.

away the freedom of German Jews to live normal lives. Hitler made more than

one _____ that would _____ the Jews, or treat them
           9.   **10.**

differently. He also sent Jews to a cruel kind of prison, or _____ .
                                                                        11.

In that terrible place, it was hard to _____ . In 1939, Hitler invaded
                                              12.

Poland. Great Britain decided to _____ Germany, and World War II
                                          13.

began. During the war years, Anne Frank, a young Jewish girl, hid with her family

in a building that had a secret _____ to the house. She wrote in
                                       14.

her diary what her life was like. She described her fears of being captured and

made a _____ of the Nazis.
              15.

126

GRAMMAR: HELPING VERBS (MODALS)

What Might Have Been . . .

Helping Verbs

In some sentences, two **helping verbs** come before a main verb to show that one action depends upon another. These sentences often use the helping verbs **would**, **could**, **should**, **might**, **may**, or **must** along with **have**.

If she had lived, Anne Frank **might have written** more books.
I **would have enjoyed** them.

DIRECTIONS Complete each sentence. Add a main verb and details.

1. In the 1940s, many German people may have _____
   felt very sad for the Jews _____ .

2. When the Franks offered Mr. Pfeffer a place to hide, he must
   have _____

   _____ .

3. Had the Franks not been discovered, they could have _____

   _____ .

4. If Anne had survived the war, she might have _____

   _____ .

DIRECTIONS Write sentences about Anne Frank. Use helping verbs from the box along with the main verb.

could have	may have	might have
must have	would have	should have

5. wished _____ Anne must have wished the war would end. _____

6. had _____

7. missed _____

8. enjoyed _____

9. wondered _____

10. talked _____

11. gotten _____

12. experienced _____

Rating Nonfiction

DIRECTIONS Evaluate a nonfiction selection.
Follow the steps.

1 Check the selection you will evaluate.

☐ "Talking Walls"   ☐ "The Great Migration"

☐ "Beyond the Color Lines" ☐ "The Big Blast"

☐ "Teammates"   ☐ "Anne Frank"

☐ "Twins"   ☐ Other: _____

> **Literary Quality**
>
> Consider these standards when you evaluate nonfiction:
> - **Clarity:** Are the ideas understandable and clear?
> - **Relevance:** Is the topic important to you?
> - **Depth:** Does the selection give details that help you understand?

2 Circle a number to rate the selection for each standard. The number 1 means the selection has low quality; 10 means it has high quality.

Standard	Rating		
Clarity	confusing, unclear	1 2 3 4 5 6 7 8 9 10	understandable, very clear
Relevance	unimportant topic	1 2 3 4 5 6 7 8 9 10	important topic
Depth	very few details	1 2 3 4 5 6 7 8 9 10	many details

3 Add the circled numbers to get a total rating for the selection. 30 is the highest rating; 3 is the lowest.

> Overall
> Rating: _____

4 Write a paragraph that evaluates the quality of the selection. Share your paragraph with a partner.

Name the selection and state your opinion of its quality.	_____ _____ _____
Tell how you rated the selection for each standard: clarity, relevance, and depth.	_____ _____ _____
Write a summary sentence about the literary quality of the selection.	_____ _____

© Hampton-Brown

Compare Events on a Time Line

The Trapp Family Singers tour the United States.

DIRECTIONS Read the passage. Complete the time line for the von Trapp family.

The von Trapp Family Singers

After his wife died, Austrian Captain Georg von Trapp hired Maria Kutschera to care for his seven children. The children loved music, so Maria taught them Austrian and German folk and religious songs.

Maria and the captain married in 1927 and life seemed perfect. During the 1930s the von Trapps sang for their friends and neighbors at local festivals to help them forget Hitler's actions in other countries. In 1937 they made their first European tour as professional singers.

This ideal life ended when Nazi soldiers invaded Austria in 1938. The family knew they could not live under Hitler's rule. Leaving all their belongings, the von Trapps escaped to Italy.

Later that same year, they emigrated to the United States, where they remained for the rest of their lives. The Trapp Family Singers performed on tour all over the United States for many years. In 1942 they settled in Stowe, Vermont.

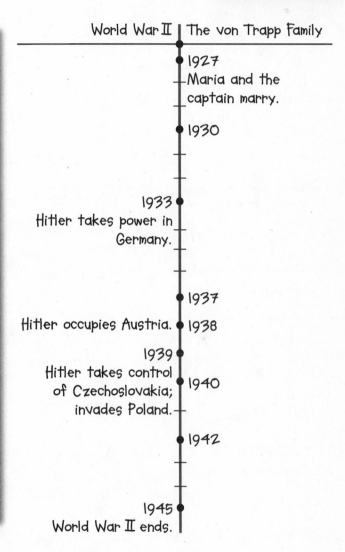

DIRECTIONS How do world events affect the lives of individuals? Answer the questions to make generalizations.

1. Were the experiences of the Franks and the von Trapps unusual during World War II? Explain.

_____

2. How did people keep their spirits up during the war?

_____

© Hampton-Brown

We Have Been Friends

DIRECTIONS Work with a partner. Be Anne or Peter. Complete your part of the dialogue. Use the present perfect tense of the verb. See Handbook pages 450–451 for a list of irregular past participles.

> **Present Perfect Tense**
> The **present perfect tense** of a verb can tell about an action that began in the past and may be still going on. It uses the helping verb **has** or **have** with the **past participle**.
> Anne and Peter **have become** friends.

(Scene: Night. Anne and Peter are sitting in the attic looking out the small window. A breeze blows in. Stars shine like chips of broken glass.)

ANNE: (*whispering*) I _____have tried_____ to get used to it here.
        1. try

PETER: Me too. I _____ myself not to think about the war.
               2. tell

ANNE: I _____ so bored! But that's not the worst thing.
             3. be

I _____ Mother and Father looking worried. They stop talking
      4. see

when they see me. Mother _____ to calm our fears.
                              5. try

PETER: My parents _____ the same way.
                      6. act

ANNE: (*upbeat, changing the mood*) I wrote some more in my diary today. Kitty

_____ me so much. My diary _____
      7. help   **8. make**

such a difference!

PETER: (*in a slightly louder voice*) Look, the stars _____ brighter.
                                              9. grow

ANNE: (*thinking*) The whole world is like the sky. Things _____
                                                               10. get

dark, but happiness may shine through. This talk _____ me up.
                                                  11. cheer

Let's find Margot. Maybe we can listen to the radio.

PETER: (*getting up*) Yes, the radio _____ another ray of hope.
                                          12. be

MORE ABOUT THE PRESENT PERFECT Practice acting out the dialogue above with your partner. Perform the scene for your class.

Nuclear Weapons Report

DIRECTIONS Work with a group. Follow the steps to research nuclear weapons.

1 **Choose Topics** Have each group member research one topic.

_____ will research the invention of the atomic bomb.

_____ will research the use and effects of the atomic bomb during World War II.

_____ will research the different types of nuclear weapons.

_____ will research which countries have nuclear weapons.

2 **Conduct Research and Cite Sources** Write facts about your topic. List the sources for your information.

Topic: _____

Facts: _____

_____

_____

_____

_____

_____

Sources: _____

_____

_____

_____

3 **Make a Chart** Show all of the topics your group researched. Write key facts. Use the chart to present your report to the class.

Topic	Key Facts
Invention of the atomic bomb	1941: Manhattan Project

4 **Give Your Report** Choose one member to give the report, or each of you may speak about a topic. As one person speaks, other members can point to facts on the chart.

Words From a Diary

Use New Words in Context

New Words

agitated

bother

call-up notice

exhausted

impression

matter

preoccupied

shock

stunned

DIRECTIONS Write the new words to complete the paragraph.
Use one new word twice.

When I read Anne Frank's diary, I get the _____ that

1.

she was a lot like me. I can feel how scared she was when her father got the

_____ . Like Anne, I try to write each memory in my

2.

personal diary. Sometimes I get so _____ over a problem

3.

that I want to scream! Instead, I write about it. That way, I am not

_____ by the situation, and I can think about other

4.

things. All of my diaries _____ more to me than anything

5.

else. I am never too _____ to write in them. One

6.

morning, I didn't even _____ to eat breakfast, because I

7.

was writing. That was a real _____ to my mother! I was

8.

_____ too when I wrote 100 pages in a month.

9.

Relate Words

DIRECTIONS Work with a partner. Choose a new word about a thought
or feeling. Role-play a scene that shows the word's meaning. Have
another pair of students guess the word.

10. agitated

11. exhausted

12. preoccupied

13. shock

14. stunned

Whose Story Is It?

DIRECTIONS Read each example of a narrator's words. Underline the pronouns. Then write the narrator's point of view.

Narrator's Point of View

> **Narrator's Point of View**
>
> The person telling a story is the narrator. The narrator uses the **first-person point of view** to tell his or her own story. The narrator uses first-person pronouns such as *I, me, my, we,* and *our.*
>   **I** felt afraid for **our** family.
>
> To tell someone else's story, a narrator uses the **third-person point of view**. The narrator uses third-person pronouns, such as *he, she, they,* or *their.*
>   **She** felt afraid for **her** family.

1. I had to tiptoe downstairs and we didn't let anyone else in. _____

2. Jews lost their jobs, and their possessions had been taken away. _____

3. Even though I knew it'd be my last night in my own bed, I fell asleep right away. _____

4. I stuck the craziest things in the bag, but I'm not sorry. Memories mean more to me than dresses. _____

5. She longed for her friends, her school, and most of all her freedom. _____

6. She wanted to be a writer. In addition to her diary, she wrote fairy tales. _____

DIRECTIONS Work with a partner. Use the first-person point of view to write about something that happened to you. Then have your partner tell the same story from the third-person point of view.

_____

_____

_____

_____

_____

_____

_____

LITERARY ANALYSIS: COMPARE LITERATURE

Anne as a Young Girl

DIRECTIONS Compare "Anne Frank" and "The Diary of a Young Girl." Complete the chart.

Anne and Margot Frank lived in Germany in 1933.

Comparing Literature

To **compare literature,** you tell how two selections are the **same** and how they are **different.** Consider these specific **attributes:**

- **Genre:** Are both selections the same type of writing?
- **Characters:** Do the same people appear in both selections?
- **Details:** Do both selections give the same details?
- **Point of View:** Are both selections told from the same point of view?

Attribute	Explanation
Genre: ☐ Same ☐ Different	
Characters: ☐ Same ☐ Different	
Details: ☐ Same ☐ Different	
Point of View: ☐ Same ☐ Different	

DIRECTIONS Write a paragraph that compares the two selections. Use information from the chart above to support your ideas. Share your paragraph with a partner.

_____

_____

_____

What Causes It?

DIRECTIONS Work with a partner to show causes and effects.

1 Review what you know about "The Diary of a Young Girl." List the most important events on each page.

	Important Events
Page 272	
Page 274	
Page 275	
Page 276	

2 Complete the chart to show the causes and effects for the important events.

Cause	→	Effect
The Franks receive a call-up notice.	→	
	→	The Franks quickly pack up their belongings.
They can't let anyone see them taking their belongings to the hiding place.	→	
	→	The house is left messy and untidy.

3 Write sentences that explain the cause-and-effect relationships.

1. The Franks receive a call-up notice so _____ .

2. The Franks quickly pack up their belongings because _____ .

3. _____

4. _____

A Place of Honor

DIRECTIONS Complete each sentence. Write the present perfect tense of the verb in parentheses. See Handbook pages 450–451 for a list of irregular past participles.

> **Present Perfect Tense**
> The **present perfect tense** of a verb can tell about an action that began in the past and may be still going on. It uses the helping verb **has** or **have** with the past participle.
>   Many people **have read** Anne Frank's diary.

1. The city of Amsterdam _____has preserved_____ the house where Anne Frank hid. (**preserve**)

2. The Anne Frank House _____ many visitors. (**welcome**)

3. Tourists _____ here from all over the world. (**come**)

4. Perhaps people _____ the presence of Anne in the rooms. (**feel**)

5. The house _____ people understand Anne's tragic situation. (**help**)

6. Visitors _____ the stairs to the secret annex. (**climb**)

7. They _____ the swinging bookcase that led to the annex. (**see**)

8. Thousands of tourists _____ into the rooms where the families hid. (**go**)

9. Because soldiers took the furniture, the rooms _____ empty for a long time. (**be**)

10. Yet Anne's movie star photos _____ on a wall. (**remain**)

11. Anne's original diary, in the permanent exhibition, _____ the hearts of many people. (**touch**)

12. Anne's spirit _____ to live. (**continue**)

Margot, Anne, and Grandma Hollander.

The Anne Frank House.

© Hampton-Brown

Explore Legacies

Franklin D. Roosevelt was
U.S. President during WWII.

DIRECTIONS Research a key figure of the World War II era.
Then role-play the person with your class.

1 **Choose a Key Figure** Write the name and title or occupation of a person from page 281 of your book.

Name: _____

Title or Occupation: _____

2 **Research and Take Notes** Look up your key figure in an encyclopedia, history book, biographical dictionary, or on the Internet. Learn about the actions and legacy of the person. Find facts that answer these questions:

• What did the leader do during World War II? _____

_____

_____

• Why were the leader's actions or contributions important? _____

_____

_____

_____

• Why should future generations learn about the leader and what the leader has done? _____

_____

_____

_____

3 **Role-Play** Review your notes. Then get together with your classmates. Pretend you are the leader you researched, and you are having dinner with other key figures of World War II.

• Ask about each leader's actions and contributions.

• Answer questions about yourself.

Example:
Albert Einstein: What do you think was your greatest contribution?
Winston Churchill: I was a strong leader when my country needed one.

Challenges

DIRECTIONS Use the mind map to write about challenges and obstacles you or others might face in life. As you read the selections in the unit, add to the map what you learn about challenges.

Challenge

Obstacles

How to Meet
the Challenge

What You
Can Learn

hard

easy

Make a Difference!

DIRECTIONS Read Kenesha's persuasive talk. Underline the verbs in the past perfect tense. For help in identifying irregular past participles, see Handbook pages 450–451.

> ## Past Perfect Tense
>
> The **past perfect tense** of a verb tells about an action that was completed before some other action in the past. It uses the helping verb **had** followed by the **past participle** of the main verb.
>
> The turtle **had waddled** across the sand
> past perfect
> before it **disappeared** into the ocean.
> past
>
> The **past participle** of regular verbs ends in **–ed**. Irregular past participles vary in their form.

The Kemp's ridley sea turtle is the most critically endangered sea turtle in the world, and you can help them right here in Texas!

Until I learned about Padre Island National Seashore on TV, I had known very little about these sea turtles. Just east of Corpus Christi, biologists were releasing rare turtle hatchlings into the sea. I headed off to help.

About 50 people had arrived at the beach before me. We all watched as biologists pulled a hundred hatchlings from a box. Eventually, two tiny hatchlings stepped toward the surf. Thirty minutes had passed since biologists put them on the sand.

During that half-hour, I learned a lot about Kemp's ridleys. In 1947, a moviemaker had filmed about 40,000 adult Kemp's ridleys nesting on a single Mexican beach in one day. By 1966, that number had dwindled to 4,000! I also learned this. Before biologists stepped in to save them, only a few of them had nested on Padre Island. Biologists had feared that one day, an oil spill or other disaster might ruin the turtles' main nesting beach in Mexico. So, they had intervened to provide a second major nesting beach at Padre Island. But back to my day at the beach!

Two hours after it all started, all of the hatchlings had waddled into the surf and they had disappeared into the Gulf of Mexico. I felt as if I had nudged a couple toward safety myself!

If you had gone with me, you would want to get involved, too. Go to Padre Island and find out how you can help!

Turtle fans show up early to cheer on the hatchlings as they take their first steps toward the sea.

© Hampton-Brown

Endangered Species Words

New Words

combat

effect

endangered

environment

extinct

ignorance

interfere

peregrine

pollution

repair

Relate Words

DIRECTIONS Complete the word map. Use the new words.

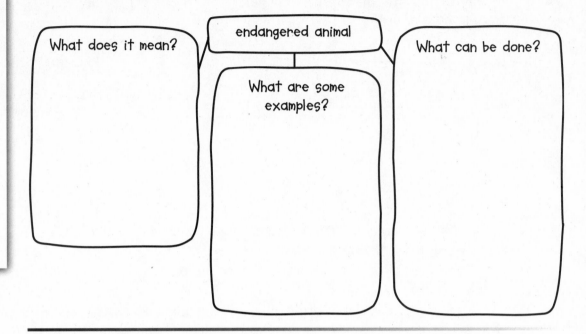

What does it mean?

endangered animal

What are some examples?

What can be done?

Use New Words in Context

DIRECTIONS Write the new words to finish the paragraph.
Write each word only once.

Garbage dumped into the _____ is called
                                  1.

_____ . Pollution results from accidents or
      2.

_____ . It is important to _____ the
      3.   **4.**

damage quickly. Even a little pollution can _____ with
                                                    5.

an environment. The _____ can be deadly for the wildlife.
                          6.

We need to help _____ species. We can
                        7.

_____ the damage. Without human help, the
      8.

_____ falcon could become _____ .
      9.   **10.**

© Hampton-Brown

GRAMMAR: PRESENT PERFECT AND PAST PERFECT TENSES

A Bird of Kings!

The endangered peregrine falcon was once the bird of kings.

> ### Present Perfect and Past Perfect Tenses
>
> The **present perfect tense** of a verb tells about an action that began in the past and may be still going on. It uses **has** or **have** followed by a **past participle**.
>
> Scientists **have kept** the eggs warm in the lab.
>
> The **past perfect tense** tells about an action that was completed before another action in the past. It uses **had** followed by a **past participle**.
>
> The chicks **had grown** healthy before scientists returned them to the nest.

DIRECTIONS Read each sentence. Underline all the verbs in the present perfect or past perfect tense.

1. Before monarchies declined, kings <u>had used</u> peregrine falcons in their hunts.

2. Once highly prized, this beautiful bird has become endangered.

3. Scientists around the world have worked hard to save peregrine falcons.

4. They have made important observations.

5. Until farmers started using DDT on their crops, the birds had laid eggs with strong shells.

6. The DDT has decreased the calcium in the birds' bodies, and the lack of calcium has made the shells of their eggs thin.

7. Peregrine chicks have died because their shells have broken under the weight of the mother bird.

8. Before DDT got into the food chain, the shells had protected the chicks until they hatched.

9. Luckily, scientists have found a way to hatch the thin eggs in laboratories.

DIRECTIONS Three sentences above use the past perfect tense. Write the sentences. Circle the verbs in the past perfect tense.

10. _____

11. _____

12. _____

GRAMMAR: ACTIVE AND PASSIVE VERBS

Vanishing Raptors

FREE SPACE!
Begin

Condors, eagles, and hawks are included in the scientific group called raptors.

passive: The scientific group "raptors" includes condors, eagles, and hawks.

Take flight!

The Endangered Species Act has helped raptor populations survive.

Capture of raptors for pets adds to the decline of raptor populations.

In the 1980s, biologists captured all the California condors and protected them in breeding programs.

Habitat destruction harms many raptors.

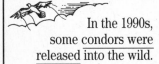 In the 1990s, some condors were released into the wild.

How to Play: *Vanishing Raptors*

1. Play in a group of three. One person is the "wildlife biologist" and uses the teacher's answer key to judge accuracy.

2. Two players choose small recycled objects as game pieces and move from space to space, taking turns. (Players jump over an occupied space.)

3. Each player reads the sentence aloud and tells whether the verb is **active** or **passive**. If the verb is passive, the player changes the verb to active and says the new sentence aloud.

4. The "biologist" counts one point for each correct response. The player with more points at *Take flight!* wins.

The eagles' nests are located in steep, forested valleys.

The species was rescued from extinction.

The bird is called the Philippine eagle.

The Puerto Rican broad-winged hawk is also endangered.

These hawks are found only in three Puerto Rican forests.

The species is threatened by timber harvest and road construction.

In 1995, the President of the Philippines declared a raptor the country's national bird.

Is This Species Endangered?

Evaluate Literature

When you **evaluate nonfiction**, consider how recent or up-to-date the source is. This can help you determine the **accuracy of information** contained in the literature.

DIRECTIONS Follow the steps to evaluate information about the California condor.

1 Look at the information Alfredo found on a Web site. Circle the date the site was last modified.

Endangered Species List - Birds

Species	Status	Range	Reasons for Decline
Condor, California	Critically Endangered	California	Habitat destruction, low reproductive rates
Parrot, orange-bellied	Endangered	Australia	Collection for pet market
Woodpecker, red-headed	Vulnerable	Southern U.S.	Nesting habitat destruction

Source: www.endangered!.com/list   Site last modified: January 1997

2 Look at the notes Alfredo took about California condors from a magazine article. Circle the date the article was written.

— November 18, 1998, The Peregrine Fund released eight California Condors in Northern Arizona.

— fourth release of the endangered species since December of 1996

Source: "California Condors Released" Condor News, December 2000

A California condor flies free.

3 Find a third source of information about California condors. Take notes. Write the title of the source and when it was created.

Source: _____   Date: _____

4 Which source is the most up-to-date? According to the most recent source, is the California condor an endangered species?   ☐ Yes   ☐ No

What's Your Conclusion?

DIRECTIONS Ask your classmates the question. Tally the
yes and *no* answers and take notes about the explanations.

	Question: Is it worth the time and money it takes to save an endangered animal?
Yes	Explanations:
No	Explanations:

DIRECTIONS Discuss the results of your poll with a group. Complete the
paragraph to summarize your discussion.

_____ members of our group think that it is worth it to save an endangered animal because
(number)

_____

_____ .

_____ members of our group think that it is not worth it to save an endangered animal because
(number)

_____

_____ .

Peregrine Rescue

DIRECTIONS Complete each sentence. Write the past perfect tense of the verb in parentheses. See Handbook pages 450–451 for a list of irregular past participles.

> ### Past Perfect Tense
>
> The **past perfect tense** of a verb tells about an action that was completed before some other action in the past. It uses the helping verb **had** followed by the <u>past participle</u> of the main verb.
>
> The climber **had** just **reached** the nest when the mother falcon saw him.
>
> The past participle of regular verbs ends in **–ed**. Irregular past participles vary in their form.

1. Lionel Cohen _____ had inspected _____ peregrine eggs before, so he knew these eggs would have trouble hatching. (**inspect**)

2. Like others he _____ , these eggs could break easily beneath the weight of a mother bird. (**see**)

3. The thinness of the shells told him that the parents

   _____ DDT. (**ingest**)

4. After the mother _____ on them for five days, he could take them to the lab. (**sit**)

5. Once she _____ this, the eggs would have a better chance of hatching. (**do**)

6. Before he arrived at the lab, Mr. Cohen

   _____ each egg. (**remove**)

7. He had replaced each egg with the kind of plaster egg that

   _____ peregrines in the past. (**fool**)

8. The scientists _____ the eggs for a month before the eggs began to hatch. (**watch**)

9. Soon healthy peregrine babies emerged from the eggs that

   Mr. Cohen _____ . (**rescue**)

10. After three weeks, the peregrine parents were able to care for the offspring that

    the scientists _____ away for a while. (**take**)

A scientist gathers eggs from a rocky cliff. Notice the eggs in the lower, right-hand corner of the photograph.

MORE ABOUT THE PAST PERFECT TENSE Write sentences from the point of view of a peregrine chick. Describe what happened to you in the laboratory. Include some verbs in the past perfect tense.

Graph Population Changes

DIRECTIONS Graph the wolf population in Yellowstone Park. Follow the steps.

1 Read the article to collect data. Circle the years and numbers.

Gray Wolves in Yellowstone Park

Gray wolves have been on the endangered species list for many years. Scientists have been tracking wolf populations in parts of the United States where the wolf population is low. Yellowstone Park in the Northern Rocky Mountains had only 14 wolves in 1995. In 1996, there were 43 wolves. In 1998, the number increased to 83. By 2000, there were 118 wolves. The gray wolf is making a comeback!

2 Make a graph. Show the wolf population in Yellowstone Park from 1995 to 2000.

- Write a title.
- Write the years on the horizontal axis.
- Fill in the bars to show the number of wolves for each year.

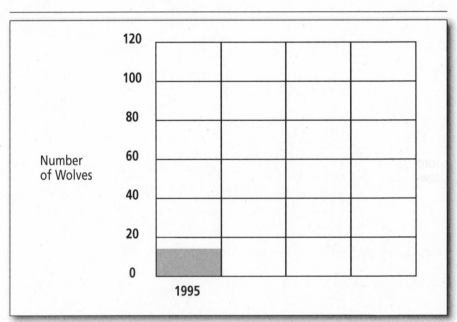

3 What does the graph tell you about the wolf population? Write your conclusion.

_____

_____

An Endangered Animal Poster

DIRECTIONS Work with a group to research an endangered species.
Follow the steps.

1 **Choose a Species** What endangered animal will your group research? _____

2 **Brainstorm Research Questions** Include questions about the animal's habitat and why it's in danger. Decide who will find facts to answer each question.

Questions   Who will research

_____   _____

_____   _____

_____   _____

3 **Research and Take Notes** Write key facts to answer your question.
Share the results with your group.

4 **Design a Poster** Discuss which facts your group will include on the poster.
Sketch what you will show.

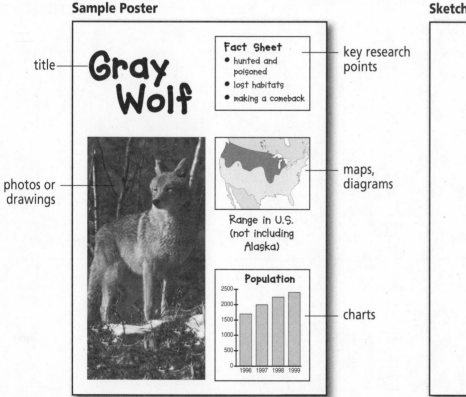

Sample Poster

title — Gray Wolf

Fact Sheet
- hunted and poisoned
- lost habitats
- making a comeback

— key research points

photos or drawings

Range in U.S. (not including Alaska)

— maps, diagrams

Population

— charts

Sketch

5 **Make the Poster** Display it in the classroom or media center.

Wetland Words

Relate Words

DIRECTIONS Complete a four-square diagram for each word.

Example:

Word: dike	Picture:
Definition: wall of stone or earth that holds back water	Sentence: The dike held back the flood waters.

Word: canal	Picture:
Definition:	Sentence:

Word: runoff	Picture:
Definition:	Sentence:

Word: extinction	Picture:
Definition:	Sentence:

Word: temperate zone	Picture:
Definition:	Sentence:

Word: levee	Picture:
Definition:	Sentence:

Word: tropics	Picture:
Definition:	Sentence:

Poetic Devices

DIRECTIONS Reread the poems on pages 317–319. Write examples of repetition and personification.

	Repetition	Personification
Some Rivers		no hurry in her
Old Man Mangrove		
Two Baby Snail Kites		

Repetition and Personification

Repetition is repeating words or phrases to create certain feelings.

Apple snails for dinner.
Apple snails for lunch.

Personification is using human traits or actions to describe things that are not human.

Baby snail kites **hope for the best**.

Baby snail kites yell for their dinner.

DIRECTIONS Use poetic devices to write a short poem about an animal. Ask a partner to identify examples of repetition and personification.

_____

_____

_____

_____

_____

Escapade in the Everglades

DIRECTIONS Read the passage. Circle the correct form of each verb.

Present and Past Perfect Tenses

The **present perfect tense** of a verb tells about an action in the past that may still be going on.

The Everglades **has existed** for thousands of years.

The **past perfect tense** tells about an action completed before another action in the past.

Before people understood the Everglades, they **had considered** it a useless swamp.

I ___have read / (had read)___ poems about the Everglades before I ever saw the
                1.

Everglades "in person." The beautiful images of slow-moving water and mangrove trees

___had made / has made___ me eager to see the real Everglades.
           2.

Since I ___has been / have been___ interested in the Everglades for a long time, I was
              3.

really excited about our trip. On the first day, we took a cruise. Seated in front, I watched the

boat slice through the glassy green water. Before we ___have been / had been___ in the boat
                                                              4.

for fifteen minutes, I ___have seen / had seen___ a blue heron and an osprey.
                            5.

The boat continued to glide past stretches of twisted mangroves. All my life I

___has dreamed / had dreamed___ of seeing a real alligator. Just as I
             6.

___had spotted / have spotted___ an egret, someone
             7.

shouted, "Look, to the left!" A huge alligator was slipping through the water!

My family and I ___had kept / have kept___ wonderful memories of our trip to the
                       8.

Everglades. We ___has thought / have thought___ about it many times. It
                       9.

___have been / has been___ a favorite story at family get-togethers. I'm so glad we went!
             10.

Responding to Literature

DIRECTIONS Review your notes about the poems on pages 317–320. Follow the steps to evaluate the literature.

1 Did the poet and the photographer achieve their purpose? State your opinion.

_____

_____

2 Find details from your notes to support your opinion. Answer the questions.

• What words expressed strong feelings?

_____

_____

• What images did the words create in your mind?

_____

_____

• How did the photographs make you feel about the Everglades?

_____

_____

3 Review "Opinion Paragraphs" on page 419 in the Handbook. Use your answers to the questions above to write an opinion paragraph.

_____

_____

_____

_____

_____

_____

4 Share your paragraph with a partner. Discuss similarities and differences.

How Are They Alike?

DIRECTIONS Read the poem. Underline the metaphors. Then complete the chart.

> **Metaphor**
>
> A **metaphor** makes a comparison by saying one thing is another thing.
>
> The river **was a silver ribbon**.
>
> A metaphor does not use the words *like* or *as*.

Night Sky
—SweetP

Her <u>moon is a lantern</u>
Swinging from east to west,

Her children are stars,
Twinkling across the sky,

Her clouds are comforters
To shelter the small ones,

Her breeze is a lullaby
From a mother's heart.

Metaphor	How One Thing is Like Another
moon is a lantern	The moon shines like a lantern.
Night is	

DIRECTIONS Work with a partner. Finish the metaphors. Then write some of your own.

Features of the Everglades	Similar Objects	Metaphors
crocodile	canoe	The crocodile was a canoe gliding on the water.
palm trees	soldiers	The palm trees are
river	rope	
grass	carpet	
sky	bowl	

WRITING: A RHYMING POEM

Rhyme Time

DIRECTIONS Follow the steps to write a rhyming poem about something in nature.

Rhyme Scheme

Rhyme scheme is the pattern of rhymes in a poem. You can mark a rhyme scheme with letters that show which lines rhyme:

Quietly munching	**a**
cow of the sea,	**b**
I confess—	**c**
I love you, manatee!	**b**

	Example	My Ideas
1. Choose a topic. List words and details that describe it.	Topic: turtle Words: moves slowly, is scaly, hard shell is home	
2. Turn the words and details into phrases or sentences.	The turtle carries his home with him. The turtle pokes his scaly head out of his front door.	
3. Arrange the lines into a logical order. Look at the words at the ends of the lines. Write letters to show which lines will rhyme.	The turtle pokes his scaly <u>head</u> a Out of his front <u>door</u>. b He carries his home with <u>him</u> c Across the sandy _____ b	
4. Brainstorm rhyming words to continue the rhyme scheme.	Words that rhyme with <u>door</u>: bore, core, floor, shore, more, store	
5. Read your poem aloud. Make changes until the rhythm is just the way you want it!	The turtle pokes his scaly head a Out from his front door. b He slowly creeps and drags his home c Across the sandy shore. b	

Evaluate Propaganda

DIRECTIONS Follow the steps to evaluate propaganda.

1 Check the propaganda technique used in each ad. Explain your choice.

> ### Propaganda
>
> **Propaganda** is used to persuade people to think, feel, or act a certain way. Propaganda uses several techniques:
>
> The **testimonial** uses well-known people to persuade you to do something.
>
> The **bandwagon** technique tells you to do something because other people are doing it.

1.

Everyone flocks to Gull Bay. Shouldn't you find out why?

☐ **bandwagon**   ☐ **testimonial**

This technique is shown by the words _____

_____ .

The ad tries to convince me to _____

_____ .

2.

Protecting our environment is an investment in our future.

—Scott Webster, Mayor of Gull Bay

☐ **bandwagon**   ☐ **testimonial**

This technique is shown by _____

_____ .

The ad tries to convince me to _____

_____ .

3.

EVERYONE CARES ABOUT GULL BAY. CARE ENOUGH TO LEND A HAND.

☐ **bandwagon**   ☐ **testimonial**

This technique is shown by _____

and the words _____ .

The ad tries to convince me to _____

_____ .

2 Do the advertisements on page 154 persuade you to do something?
Check *yes* or *no* for each question.

		Yes	No
Ad 1	Does the picture make Gull Bay seem attractive?		
	Do the words make Gull Bay seem attractive?		
	Does the ad make you want to go to Gull Bay?		
Ad 2	Do you think the mayor would know what is best for Gull Bay?		
	Does the picture make you want to protect places like Gull Bay?		
	Do the words make you want to protect places like Gull Bay?		
Ad 3	Does the picture make you want to join the crowd?		
	Do the words make you want to help out?		
	Do you agree that everyone cares?		
	The most effective ad is _____ .		

3 Collect examples of ads and evaluate them. Complete the chart.

Medium and Product	Technique	Effectiveness
– magazine – Power Grain Bars	testimonial	It is effective because a great athlete says the bars are good for you. He should know about foods that are healthy to eat.

Using an Atlas and Globe

DIRECTIONS Look at the climate map of the eastern part of the United States. Answer the questions.

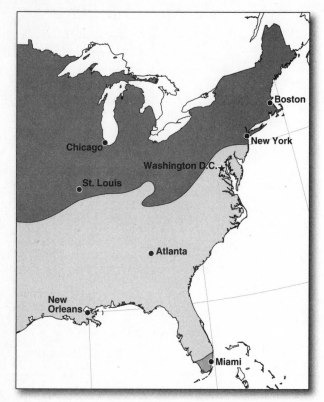

 Humid continental
Mild summers and cold winters

 Humid subtropical
Warm to hot summers and cool winters

 Tropical wet and dry
Always hot, with alternate wet and dry seasons

Atlas and Globe

An **atlas** is a book of maps. An atlas shows physical and political maps. It may contain specialized maps that show such things as population, vegetation, transportation, language, and climate.

A **globe** is a three-dimensional model of Earth. A globe usually shows continents, borders, major cities, landforms, and bodies of water.

Globe

1. What is the difference between summers in Chicago and Atlanta? _____

_____

2. What is the climate of New Orleans? _____

3. What is the climate of Miami? _____

4. In which climate do you think it snows the most? Explain. _____

_____

5. Why do you think Chicago's climate is cooler than Miami's? _____

_____

6. Ghana is in Africa. India is in Asia. Both countries have the same climate as the

southern tip of Florida. Find them on a globe. What can you say about their

distance from the equator? _____

BUILD LANGUAGE AND VOCABULARY

Tell More About Survival

DIRECTIONS Work with a small group. Imagine that you have made an emergency landing in the wilderness before dawn.

1 **Discuss Your Ideas** Think about the topics in the box. How will you provide these necessities?

2 **Complete Each Sentence** Use the future perfect tense. See Handbook pages 450–451 for a list of irregular past participles.

3 **Share Your Work** Read your group's sentences aloud to other groups. Listen to what the other groups would do. How will each group have pushed past the limits?

Future Perfect Tense

The **future perfect tense** of a verb tells about an action that will be completed at a specific time in the future. It uses the helping verbs **will have** followed by the **past participle** of the main verb.

By nightfall, we **will have eaten** little.

safety	shelter	fuel for fire
water	food	message for help

1. By the time the plane catches fire, _everyone will have jumped out of it_ _____

_____.

2. By sunrise, _____

_____.

3. After a few hours, _____

_____.

4. Shortly after that, _____

_____.

5. By noon, _____

_____.

6. By late afternoon, _____

_____.

7. Soon after that, _____

_____.

8. By the time a rescue plane comes, _____

_____.

Migrant Labor Words

Locate and Use Definitions

DIRECTIONS Guess the meaning of each new word. Then write
the Glossary definition. Make a check if your guess was correct.

Word	What I Think It Means	What It Really Means	✔
camp foreman	head person in a camp	person in charge of the workers in a camp	✔
crate			
enroll			
grape season			
labor camp			
migrant worker			
shack			
vineyard			
year-round job			

Use Words in Context

DIRECTIONS Use each new word in a sentence. You may use two
new words in one sentence.

1. _____

2. _____

3. _____

4. _____

5. _____

6. _____

7. _____

8. _____

GRAMMAR: PAST PERFECT AND FUTURE PERFECT TENSES

Another Move

DIRECTIONS Complete the passage. Use the correct form of the verb. See Handbook pages 450–451 for a list of irregular past participles.

> **Past Perfect and Future Perfect Tenses**
>
> The **past perfect tense** of a verb tells about an action that was completed before some other action in the past. It uses the helping verb **had** followed by a **past participle**.
>
> Serena **had <u>risen</u>** before dawn.
>
> The **future perfect tense** tells about an action that will be completed at a specific time in the future. It uses the helping verbs **will have** followed by a **past participle**.
>
> By dinnertime, she **will have <u>made</u>** new friends.

The Perez family _____had moved_____
          1. move; past perfect

into their new home over the weekend. "I thought I

_____ used to
     2. get; past perfect

moving," Serena said at breakfast on Monday. "But I haven't." She took a bite of *pan dulce*.

"By the time I am fifteen, I _____ a thousand times! I
                         3. move; future perfect

_____ in twenty-five schools!" Serena went on. "By tonight,
    4. enroll; future perfect

I _____ at a hundred strange new faces—again!"
    5. look; future perfect

"And," said Mami, "you _____ several new friends."
           6. meet; future perfect

"But I _____ the perfect friends at my last high school,
       7. make; past perfect

and I _____ the perfect teacher!" complained Serena.
      8. find; past perfect

"I know it is hard," said Mami. "But by the time you have graduated,

you _____ many things. You
      9. learn; future perfect

_____ something in each place."
    10. acquire; future perfect

"I hadn't thought of that," said Serena, kissing Mami goodbye, as

she _____ hundreds of times
      11. do; past perfect

before. "By tonight, I _____
      12. do; future perfect

it again!"

By the end of the day, Serena will have proven her courage once again.

Life Messages

DIRECTIONS Work with a partner to relate stories to a theme.

1 Review "Amir" on pages 116–122 in your book. Then complete the sentences.

> **Theme**
>
> The **theme** of a story is its message about life or human nature. To explain a message about life, a writer tells what characters in the story have learned. Several stories can relate to the same theme in different ways.

1. When she got to know Amir, the Italian woman _____

_____ .

2. The author's message about life is that getting to know other people

can _____ .

2 Read the story below and complete the sentences.

Yhsa

One winter, the village ran out of food. The villagers sat in huddled groups, not knowing what to do. Then Yhsa picked up a shovel and began to dig.

"What do you think you are doing, foolish Yhsa," the villagers growled, "digging at a time like this?" Silently, Yhsa began to throw roots into a pot. Soon a delicious smell floated through the air.

"What have you done, wise Yhsa?" the villagers cried as they lined up eagerly to fill their bowls. "How have you brought food from the dirt?"

"I just looked deeper," was the reply.

3. The villagers learned that _____

_____ .

4. The author's message about life is that _____

_____

3 Choose one theme for both stories. Then complete the theme map.

Theme:

| How "Amir" relates to the theme: | How "Yhsa" relates to the theme: |

Unique Responses

DIRECTIONS Ask two people outside your class to read "The Circuit" and answer the questions. Write the responses. Discuss them with a partner.

> **Responses to Literature**
>
> Each person's **response to literature** is unique. No response is wrong. Your responses come from your past experiences, your opinions, and your feelings.

Questions	_____'s Responses	_____'s Responses
How do you feel about Panchito? Explain.		
How do you feel about Panchito's family? Explain.		
How do you feel about Mr. Lema? Explain.		

DIRECTIONS Compare the two responses. Tell how you think each person's experiences, opinions, and feelings affected his or her responses.

_____

_____

_____

_____

Compare Causes and Effects

DIRECTIONS Get ready to compare "Twins" and "The Circuit."
Complete the cause-and-effect chains for "Twins."

The Silent Years, pages 160–161

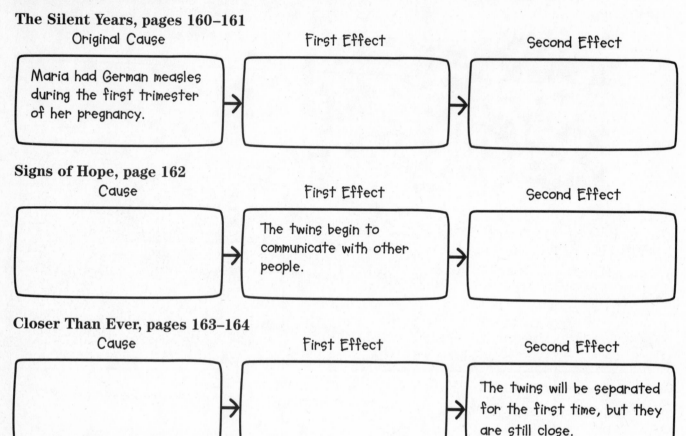

Original Cause

Maria had German measles during the first trimester of her pregnancy.

First Effect

Second Effect

Signs of Hope, page 162

Cause

First Effect

The twins begin to communicate with other people.

Second Effect

Closer Than Ever, pages 163–164

Cause

First Effect

Second Effect

The twins will be separated for the first time, but they are still close.

DIRECTIONS Review the cause-and-effect chain for "The Circuit." Write a paragraph that compares the causes and effects in "Twins" and "The Circuit." Describe the twins' and Panchito's families, tell what changes and challenges they faced, and describe how they responded. Discuss your comparison with a group.

_____

_____

_____

_____

_____

GRAMMAR: FUTURE PERFECT TENSE

In the Vineyards

DIRECTIONS Read the article. Then complete each sentence. Use a verb in the future perfect tense.

Future Perfect Tense

The **future perfect tense** of a verb tells about an action that will be completed at a specific time in the future. It uses the helping verbs **will have** followed by a **past participle**.

By November, the grape season **will have ended**.

How Grapes Are Planted and Grown

Grapes grow in clusters on grapevines. During the winter, workers clip branches off the woody vines. They snip the branches into sections, or cuttings, and store them under sand. When spring comes, the workers move the cuttings to nurseries. The following spring they plant the cuttings, which have grown roots, in vineyards. There, the rooted cuttings grow into vines.

A year after that, workers prop up, or support, the young vines with posts and wires. As the vines grow, they coil around the wires. Growers harvest grapes from summer into autumn. They trim the vines each year at pruning time. Grapevines are usually ready to produce a partial crop after three or four years. It takes several years before a vineyard produces a full crop of grapes.

Workers harvest grapes in Napa Valley, California.

1. By the end of winter, workers _____will have clipped_____ branches off the vines.

2. Before the first spring is over, the workers _____ the cuttings to nurseries.

3. By the end of the second spring, the workers _____ the cuttings in vineyards.

4. A year after that, workers _____ the young vines.

5. By the end of each pruning season, workers _____ the vines.

6. Within three or four years, the grapevines _____ at least a partial crop.

7. By the middle of each autumn, growers _____ grapes.

8. After several years, the vineyard _____ a full crop.

Use Logical Order

DIRECTIONS Study each writing form. Answer the questions.

News Article

The lead paragraph answers the questions *Who? What? Where? When? Why?* and *How?*

More facts are given in the body of the article.

> ### Jiménez Graduates with Honors
>
> Francisco Jiménez graduated with honors today from Santa Clara University in California. It was a goal he had worked hard to achieve.
>
> It was difficult for Jiménez to get an education. As a child, he worked in the fields and he could not always attend school. His family moved constantly from one farming community to another. In spite of all this, he did very well in his studies and he received several college scholarships.

1. What did you learn from the first paragraph? _____

_____

2. Read this fact: His family had to move to find work.
   Does this fact belong in the first or second paragraph? Why? _____

_____

Description of a Place

Details are described in order from front to back, left to right, or top to bottom.

> ### Our House
>
> The small garage we live in is worn out. The front wall is a creaky door that swings up. It had termite holes in it, but Papá patched them with tin can tops. Just inside the door there are boxes of clothes against both side walls. In the middle of the hard dirt floor are four wooden crates that we use for chairs and a table. On the back wall is a shelf with a few pots and pans on it. An old mattress is under it. The garage has no windows, so I drew a picture of a window and taped it on the back wall. It shows a view of the ocean.

3. How does the writer help you visualize the garage? _____

_____

_____

Persuasive Letter

A persuasive letter states an opinion first and gives a reason for writing.

Next, the writer adds supporting details and reasons for the opinion.

Finally, the writer tells what actions he or she wants the reader to take.

> Dear Congressman Smith:
>
> I think employers should provide better housing for farm workers. Please propose a law that will require this.
>
> Our homes are small. They have no heaters or air conditioners. Doors, walls, and floors are damaged. The plumbing and electricity need to be repaired.
>
> With better housing, we would be safer, healthier, and happier. We would also be more productive workers.
>
> Please propose a law to Congress that requires employers to provide good living conditions for farm workers.

4. How does the writer feel about housing for farm workers? _____

_____

DIRECTIONS Choose a writing form. Then write your article, description, or letter.

☐ **News Article** Write about Panchito's graduation from college.

☐ **Scene Description** Describe a place from "The Circuit."

☐ **Persuasive Letter** Suggest ways to improve life for farm workers. You might write to an employer or teacher.

_____

_____

_____

_____

_____

_____

_____

_____

_____

_____

Using Maps

DIRECTIONS Use latitude and longitude lines to find each place on the map. Draw a crop symbol to show the location.

1. Walnuts are grown at 38°N, 121°W.

2. Sugar beets are grown at 33°N, 115°W.

3. Vegetables are grown at 36°N, 121°W.

4. Fruit is grown at 40°N, 122°W.

5. Cotton is grown at 35°N, 119°W.

6. Grapes are grown at 37°N, 120°W.

Latitude and Longitude

On a map, horizontal lines tell the **latitude**, or the distance north or south of the equator.

Vertical lines tell the **longitude**, or the distance east or west of the prime meridian.

Trees for forest products are grown at 41°N, 121°W.

In California, trees are grown 41 degrees north of the equator (latitude) and 121 degrees west of the prime meridian (longitude).

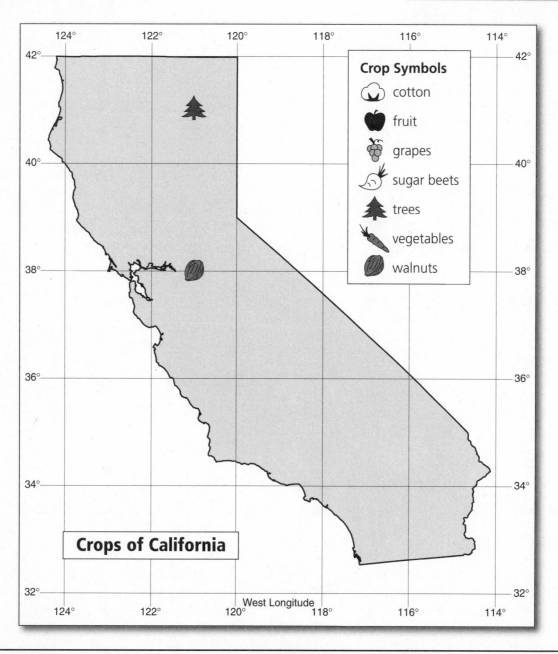

Crop Symbols

- cotton
- fruit
- grapes
- sugar beets
- trees
- vegetables
- walnuts

Crops of California

West Longitude

Words About Stairs

Use Words in Context

New Words

board
crystal
landing
splinter
stair
tack

DIRECTIONS Use the new words to describe stairs.
Write one sentence on each step.

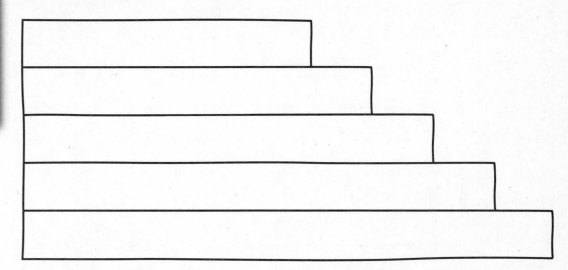

Relate Words

DIRECTIONS Complete the Venn diagram to compare a crystal stair and
a wooden one. Use the new words and words of your own.

Crystal Stair

is expensive

Both

Wooden Stair

is not expensive

Degrees of Meaning

New Words

appalling arrogance

boastful

braggart

capability

cleverness

conceited

incomparable wisdom

matchless wit

remarkably proud

swollen head

unusually clever

Sort Words

DIRECTIONS Work with a partner. Complete the T-chart.

Words that tell about capability, or how able a person is:	Words that tell about a swollen head, or how proud a person is:
incomparable wisdom	appalling arrogance
_____	_____
_____	_____
_____	_____

Relate Words

DIRECTIONS Discuss the example with your partner. Then use your T-chart above to complete the diagram.

Example:
How wet was the shirt?

dripping (so full that water is dripping out of it)
soaked (full of water)
moist (wet to the touch)
damp (almost dry)

Degrees of Wetness

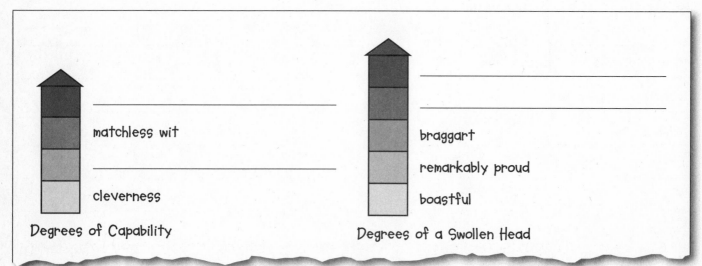

matchless wit

_____

cleverness

Degrees of Capability

braggart

remarkably proud

boastful

Degrees of a Swollen Head

© Hampton-Brown

LITERARY ANALYSIS: ONOMATOPOEIA

Sound Off!

DIRECTIONS Read the poem. Look at the underlined examples of onomatopoeia. What noises do they sound like?

Onomatopoeia

Onomatopoeia is using words that imitate the sounds of the things they describe.

"Awk!" screamed the peregrine falcon.

Sounds Like Silverstein and Seuss

— P. Edwards

Some poets love to zap us
  with sounds.
Their characters never just drink;
They have to slurp.
Their dogs don't bark;
They always woof or yap!
When the flu is going around,

Can't people just sneeze?
Must everyone kerchoo?
Some poets like to whack us
With plops of noise,
buzz!
roar!
hiss…

1. *zap*: _____lightning or electricity_____

2. *slurp*: _____

3. *woof*: _____

4. *yap*: _____

5. *kerchoo*: _____

6. *whack*: _____

7. *plops*: _____

8. *buzz*: _____

9. *roar*: _____

10. *hiss*: _____

DIRECTIONS Work with a partner. What noise does each word sound like? Use each onomatopoeia in a sentence.

Onomatopoeia	Sounds Like	Sentence
beep		
click		
crunch		
howl		
thump		

What Have You Got to Lose?

DIRECTIONS Read the story. Complete the sentences.

> **Characterization**
>
> The **protagonist** is the character with the most to gain or lose by the outcome of the story. Characters who have less to gain or lose are called **minor characters**.

The Class Trip

Stephi wanted to go on the class trip. When she asked her father about it, however, he said, "It's pretty expensive. You'll have to earn half the money yourself."

How could she earn so much money in such a short time? Stephi sat sadly on the porch, dreaming of the trip she would miss.

Trevor, Stephi's little brother, heard what Dad said. Trevor would do anything to please Stephi, but he felt too small to make a difference. His great ideas usually seemed to fall apart and he always felt awful. Maybe this time he would think of a good plan and become Stephi's hero. He crept up quietly beside his sister. "I have a good idea," he said, softly.

"Oh, Trevor," Stephi said. "You always have good ideas but they never seem to work out. Then, seeing his face, she went on, "Okay, let's hear your plan."

"Well," Trevor smiled. "Mr. Chavez needs someone to water his plants while he's gone and Mrs. Vu needs…"

Three weeks later, Stephi handed her father more than half the amount needed for the class trip. "Wow! I'm really proud of you, Stephi. I'll be happy to cover the rest," Dad said.

"It was really Trevor's idea," Stephi said. "Thanks, Hero," she whispered in Trevor's ear. Her brother's shoulders seemed a little broader after that.

1. The protagonist is _____ .

   I know this because _____ .

   This character has a lot to gain because _____ .

   This character has a lot to lose because _____ .

2. The minor characters are _____ .

   I know this because _____ .

   They have less to gain because _____ .

Summary Steps

DIRECTIONS Read the story. Write the important details and a summary statement for each part.

Make Him Laugh

A Woman Goes to Town

One day a woman set out to sell her goat. "I am going to the village," she told her sick husband. "What can I bring you, Dear?"

"Bring some eggs and something to make me laugh," her husband replied. "Laughing always makes me feel better."

"Yes, it does" the woman agreed with a sad smile.

The Husband Works at Home

While his wife was gone, the husband mended some clothes and cooked a pot of soup. He wondered what his wife would bring to make him laugh.

The Woman Returns

"My Dear! Where are the eggs?" the man asked, when his wife returned, leading the goat.

"I did buy eggs," she sighed. "But when I started home, I realized I had not sold the goat. On the way back to the market, the goat ran off. I chased her and dropped the eggs. By the time I caught her, the market was closed. So here I am with the goat, without the eggs, and with nothing to make you laugh."

A big smile spread across her husband's face. "What a great story," he chuckled. "You made me laugh and I feel better already."

A Woman Goes to Town	The Husband Works at Home	The Woman Returns
Details:	Details:	Details:
Summary Statement:	Summary Statement:	Summary Statement:

DIRECTIONS Use your section summaries to summarize the entire story. Share your summary with a group.

_____

_____

_____

LANGUAGE ARTS CONNECTION

How Setting Affects Characters

DIRECTIONS Study the setting for "The Clever Wife." Complete the chart to show how each element of the setting affected the thoughts and actions of the characters.

Setting
The **setting** of a story is where and when the events happen. If you understand the setting, you know more about the characters and the events in the plot.

Setting: The Clever Wife

Elements in the Setting: China During the Han Dynasty	Effects on the Characters
The government encourages intelligent and educated thinking.	
The magistrate could punish people by killing them.	
Any family member could be punished for the actions of another family member.	

DIRECTIONS Work with a partner. How would Fu-hsing and the other characters think and act in a different setting? Brainstorm how each element below would affect the characters. Then write a paragraph that summarizes your ideas.

Elements in a New Setting
- The story takes place on Planet Ximpha in the year 2405.
- Only members of the government are allowed to be intelligent.
- The government encourages stupidity among the common people. Each year it awards the Great Seal of Endless Wealth to the least intelligent people and their families.

_____

_____

_____

_____

WRITING: A STORY REVIEW

What Did You Think of It?

DIRECTIONS Follow the steps to write a review of "The Clever Wife." Revise your draft. Then share your final review with the class.

The Clever Wife

Write the title and authors' names. Tell the main idea of the story. Summarize the important events.

_____

_____

_____

_____

_____

_____

_____

Tell how you feel about the story and why.

_____

_____

_____

_____

_____

_____

_____

Tell the most important idea you learned from the story. End with a sentence that sums up your ideas.

_____

_____

_____

_____

_____

The Clever Wife
LEVEL B TE page T355

Acknowledgments

Every effort has been made to secure permission, but if any omissions have been made, please let us know. We gratefully acknowledge the following permissions:

p 13: Copyright © 1989 by Houghton Mifflin Company. Adapted and reproduced by permission from Houghton Mifflin Intermediate Dictionary.

p 16: From THE SUN GIRL AND THE MOON BOY by Yangsook Choi. Copyright © 1997 by Yangsook Choi. Used by permission of Alfred A. Knopf Children's Books, a division of Random House, Inc.

p 28: Excerpted from THE WORLD BOOK ENCYCLOPEDIA. © 1998 World Book, Inc. By permission of the publisher. www.worldbook.com

p 44: From the New American Roget's College Thesaurus, © 1985, prepared by Philip D. Morehead. Published by the Penguin Group. Used by permission.

p 51: Reprinted with permission from The World Almanac for Kids 2000. Copyright © 1999 World Almanac Education Group. All rights reserved.

Photographs:

AG Stock: p 22 (wheat, © John M. Lund)
AP/Wide World Photos: p 121 (Armero, © AP/Wide World Photo), p 47 (Satchel Paige, © AP/Wide World Photo)
Archive Photos: p87 (woman, © Archive Photo), p140 (man and woman, © Archaeological Museum, Ferrara, Italy / ET Archive, London/Superstock)
CORBIS: p 49 (Wilma Rudolph, © Bettman/Corbis), p 78 (twins, © Corbis), p 88 (miner, © Bettman/Corbis), p 111 (winter carnival, © Neil Rabinowitz) p 141 (Peregrine falcon nest, © John Hawkins / Frank Lane Picture Agency), p 145 (scientist, © Galen Rowell), p 154 (man, © Roger Ressmeyer), p 154 (Gull Bay, © Catherine Karnow), p 127 (Anne Frank's bookcase, © Wolfgang Kaehler)
Janjaap Dekker: pp 4-5 (Gary Soto, © Janjaap Dekker)
Dell Publishing, a division of Random House, Inc.: p 159, 163 (Neshmayda and Suzette, copyright © 1998 by Bill Ballenberg. Used by permission of Dell Publishing, a division of Random House, Inc.)
Digital Stock: p 101 (cityscape, © Digital Stock)
FPG International: p 154 (beach clean up, © Arthur Tilley)
Holiday House, Inc.: p 43 (Janell, © 1997 by Robert Crum. All rights reserved.)
Hulton Getty / Archive Photos: (All photos © Hulton Getty / Archive Photo) p 88 (San Francisco), p 91 (Harriet Tubman), p 125 (British Spitfire), p 133 (Anne Frank and Margot, © Anne Frank Fonds, Basel/ Anne Frank House, Amsterdam/ Archive Photo), p 137 (Franklin D. Roosevelt), p 127 (Anne Frank, © Anne Frank Fonds, Basel/ Anne Frank House, Amsterdam/ Archive Photo)
The Image Works: p 136 (Anne Frank's house, © Topham / The Image Works)
International Stock: p 103 (Acropolis, © Michael Gerard), p 146 (gray wolf, © Bob Jacobson), p 153 (turtle, © Roger Marckham-Smith)

Ted Levin: p 149 (snail kites, © Ted Levin)
Leah Missbach: p 95 (Esperanza, © Leah Missbach)
Richard Morganstein: p 17 (Diane Ferlatte, © Richard Morgenstein)
The Museum of Modern Art, New York, and the Phillips Collection: p 81 (The Studio. Paris [winter 1927-28; dated 1928]. Oil on canvas, 59" x 7'7" [149.9 x 231.2 cm] ©The Museum of Modern Art, New York. Gift of Walter P. Chrysler, Jr. Photograph © 2000 The Museum of Modern Art, New York, ARS, New York.), p 84 (© 1993 by The Museum of Modern Art, New York, and the Phillips Collection. Used by permission of HarperCollins Publishers.
PhotoEdit: p 37 (nesting dolls, © Felicia Martinez), p 77 (raft, © Bonnie Kamin), p 159 (girl, © D. Young Wolff MR), p 160 (Malik, © David K. Crow), p 163 (vineyard, © Mark Richards)
Photo File Inc.: p 46 (Roberto Clemente, © Photo File Inc.)
Photo Researchers: p 143 (California Condor, © John Borneman)
Sacramento Train Museum: p 82 (train, © Dan Polin)
San Antonio Express News: p 139 (Turtle Fans, © Kin Man Hui), p 139 (sea turtle, © Kin Man Hui)
The Stock Market: p 106 (gardening, © Joh Feingersh), p 110 (mountain bikers, © 1997 Bill Miles), p 166 (cotton plant, © 1999 Wes Thompson)
Superstock: p 2 (I and the Village, © Museum of Modern Art, New York, Marc Chagall)
Stone: p 43 (petroglyphs, © David Hiser), p 64 (pig, © Tim Davis)
University of New Mexico: p 97 (Mary Helen Ponce, © Yvon Douvan)
USGS Cascades Volcano Observatory: p 124 (volcano, © USGS Cascades Volcano Observatory)
The von Trapp Family Lodge: p 129 (von Trapp family, © von Trapp Family Lodge)
Roger Weurth: p 118 (Bud May, © Roger Werth / Longview Washington Daily News)

Illustrations:

Priscilla Burris: pp 24, 25, 27
Len Epstein: pp 105, 130
Merilee Heyer: p 70
Pamela Johnson: pp 31, 33, 35, 50, 60, 69
Kathleen Kinkopf: pp 54, 55
Judy Love: pp 8, 18, 26, 48, 112, 113, 114, 115, 170, 171
Russel Nemec: pp 111, 123, 147, 156, 166
Rik Olson: pp 99, 142, 151, 169
Jean and Mou-sien Tseng: p 173
Joel Snyder: p 11
Simon and Schuster Books: p 34 (Reprinted by permission of Simon and Schuster Books for Young Readers, an imprint of Simon and Schuster Children's Publishing from THE KEEPING QUILT by Patricia Polacco. Copyright © 1988 Patricia Polacco.)
Lane Yerkes: pp 67, 99

Hampton-Brown Staff Credits

Editorial Staff: Susan Blackaby, Kellie Crain, Phyllis Edwards, Suzanne Gardner, Fredrick Ignacio, Barbara Linde, Dawn Liseth, Daphne Liu, Sheron Long, Michele McFadden, Elizabeth Sengel, Sharon Ursino, Andreya Valabek, Lynn Yokoe

Design and Production Staff: Marcia Bateman Walker, Matthew Brown, Andrea Carter, Connie DeLa Garza, Lauren Grace, Davis Hernandez, Russell Nemec, Debbie Saxton, Curtis Spitler, Margaret Tisdale, JR Walker

Permissions Staff: Barbara Mathewson